Gardening on the Menu

MARTIN and JILL FISH

2QT Limited (Publishing)

2QT Limited (Publishing)
Settle
North Yorkshire
BD24 9RH
United Kingdom

Reprinted in 2020

First Edition printed in 2017

Cover, gardening and cookery images: Martin and Jill Fish

Printed in Italy by Printer Trento Srl.

A CIP catalogue record for this book is available from the British Library

ISBN 978-1-912014-56-9

This book is dedicated to our mums – Betty the original 'good little cooker' and Joyce the 'champion scone baker'.

When we are giving our 'Gardening on the Menu' talk, we always get such lovely feedback and have had numerous requests for a book. So, here we go – hope you enjoy it!

To Mike,

Happy gardening

Good cooking

Foreword - Carol Klein

What a welcome and original addition to the long list of books on growing and eating. What immediately strikes you is that this book is packed full of practical information, common sense - and inspiration. Years of Martin's planting and harvesting and Jill's cooking, baking and preserving, have given these pages a trustworthiness and credibility that will keep you returning to them year after year.

The message is clear - grow to eat. Each makes the other more enjoyable!

The photos illustrate exactly what is going on and when you read Martin's words it is clear he is passing on his everyday practice refined after many years of experience. He tells you what he does and you know it's going to work for you. You feel confident to go out there and sow your beans, plant your cabbages or even harvest your asparagus! Everything is covered.

Martin's tips, dotted through the text/pages, are little nuggets of wisdom; they all hit the horticultural nail on the head.

You know when you follow one of Jill's recipes it is easy, straightforward and the results are going to be delicious.

Good gardening and good cooking should not be slaves to fashion, they rise above trendiness, and though Martin and Jill's book is bang up to date the quality of their knowledge and their ability to transmit it will be relevant indefinitely.

You'll learn everything you need to know about growing your own veg and even when you've been doing it for years, you'll read these pages and think, just as I have, "Thanks Martin. That's a better way to do that. I'm going to do it like that in future ... and thanks, Jill. I can't wait to taste that!"

A final thought, when a woman like me from the other side of the Pennines extols the product of a Yorkshire garden, you know it must be good.

Contents

Introduction

Martin

One of the things I enjoy about gardening is being able to wander into our garden and pick fresh fruit and vegetables. Even after many years of growing, it still gives me a great sense of satisfaction to think that I've grown the vegetables on our dinner plates!

I have been gardening professionally since I started as an apprentice when I was sixteen years old, but my love of gardening goes back even further to when I gardened as a child. It started in my Grandma Smith's traditional cottage garden in Nottinghamshire and with my Uncle Colin, who grew vegetables and kept a few hens and ducks on Grandma's large back garden. I remember spending hours in the garden with him and when I was around twelve years old we built a very basic greenhouse out of old wood and polythene and grew a crop of tomatoes. Every year when I plant tomatoes out in my own greenhouse, I'm instantly taken back.

A few years later I also helped out on the allotment with my Uncle Arthur. He was a miner at the village pit and like many other miners, his hobby was allotment gardening. He also did a bit of exhibiting at local garden shows, especially onions. By the time I was fifteen, I had my own allotment next to his, although I seem to remember my uncle did a lot of the work for me, especially the weeding! Looking back, it was those early experiences of gardening with family and growing vegetables that set me on a career as a gardener.

Left above: The vegetable plot at Thornycroft
Below: The garden and summer house

Left: Jill and her jam pan.
Below: Martin getting ready for the National Garden Scheme day at Thornycroft

Jill

When I got together with Martin over twenty years ago, I'd really only ever grown a few bits and bobs of fruit and veg for myself. Maybe a tomato plant and some strawberries along with some herbs on my back doorstep.

Suddenly I found myself being bombarded with fruit and veg every day in the kitchen and discovered that the taste of ingredients straight from the plot is really second to none – my favourites have to be asparagus and ... raspberries, I think! I quickly started collecting recipes from everywhere – my mum and Joyce (my mother-in-law), friends, magazines and cook books – and tried to make the most of the regular harvests. I 'borrowed' mum's jam pan and developed a love of jamming, then experimented with bottling, pickling and preserving in all sorts of ways.

We had three children and wanted them to eat as healthily as possible so almost every meal had fruit or veg in it somewhere and they were always welcome to go and pick things to eat straight out of the garden. Aimee was always picking strawberries, Richard loved cherry tomatoes warm from the greenhouse and Harriet always wanted cabbage for tea!

Now, of course, it's just the two of us but Martin still seems to grow just as much, so the cupboards are always groaning under the weight of jars and bottles of this and that. Everyone gets a hamper for Christmas!

The recipes in this book are some of our family favourites that we've been cooking for years, along with some quick tips and ideas that you may find useful. Please don't expect perfection though – I'm not trained in any way other than feeding my family.

The garden at Thornycroft

In the spring of 2009 Jill and I moved to our new home in a North Yorkshire village. The house stands on around three quarters of an acre and the vegetable plot was the first part of the garden we set out. I was writing about growing fruit and vegetables for ***Garden News*** and Jill was writing the cookery page each week and, having left an established garden in Nottinghamshire, we needed to get a veg plot going straight away! To start with it was very simple and all we did was mark out the growing beds, lift the turf and cultivate the ground. The paths between the beds were left as grass and mown weekly to keep the area tidy. We also fenced the plot off, partly to keep it separate from the rest of the garden, but also because at the time we had a yellow Labrador called Ellie who loved eating fruit and veg! She really knew the benefits of five a day and if allowed into the garden, would graze on cabbages and eat all the soft fruit. Molly, our other dog, also likes fresh produce, although she much prefers apples and pears to raw vegetables.

The vegetable garden is a formal layout that is divided into four main growing beds which are rotated each year, plus borders around the edge where we grow soft fruit, rhubarb and asparagus. We've now replaced the grass paths with brick edging and gravel to give it a more decorative feel and of course it saves time on grass cutting!

To extend the growing season, a small polytunnel and greenhouse enable us to start a month earlier in spring and to carry on cropping well into autumn, and this has proved invaluable over the past few years.

We also planted a small orchard of sixteen trees consisting mainly of apple, plus pear, plum and damson trees. There's a mixture of heritage and modern varieties, such as the famous Nottinghamshire 'Bramley's Seedling', but also some Yorkshire apples with 'Ribston Pippin' being one of them. Not only do the trees unite the counties where we were both born and now live, but they are also all grown because they are good apples that taste delicious.

We try to garden as naturally as possible, but we don't claim to be totally organic. I certainly don't spray anything that we eat with chemicals, but I will use natural, organic insecticides if needed. We make as much garden compost as possible using vegetable and garden waste, supplemented by manure from my hens, and this is used along with well-rotted manure and mushroom compost to help keep the soil in good condition. Compost and manure on their own do not supply enough nutrients for most vegetables, so I also use a general fertiliser on the plots. The theory is to feed the soil, which in turn feeds the plants. Our soil is a lovely sandy loam that drains well but also retains moisture, meaning we can grow a wide range of plants. Having gardened on heavy clay for twenty years in Nottinghamshire, the soil at Thornycroft is an absolute delight to garden on.

From our plot we could be self-sufficient. What isn't eaten fresh is stored, frozen or turned into wonderful jams, chutneys and pickles by Jill. Although we could manage on what we grow, we choose to buy different vegetables that we either can't or don't grow to give us more variety through the year. However, we are both advocates of only eating what is in season and in a way that's what makes growing your own so special. It's always a bit of a shame when one crop comes to the end of its season but exciting that another will follow on to provide us with a lovely selection of fresh and tasty home-grown produce all through the year.

The garden is now well established and as well as providing us with a good selection of fresh fruit and vegetables, it doubles up as a workplace for my writing for *Kitchen Garden* magazine, *Garden News*, *Which? Gardening* and other publications. I also regularly broadcast from the garden, greenhouse or potting shed as part of my radio work for BBC Radio Nottingham and BBC Radio York.

The veg plot is just part of the larger garden that has now been set out as a series of beds and borders to create an informal country garden. We open the garden to raise money for the National Garden Scheme and also for group visits through the summer months.

Gardening is all about growing what you want and that's exactly what we do in our garden. This book certainly isn't intended as an encyclopaedic A–Z of growing and cooking fruit and vegetables and unfortunately we've had to miss some out. But, we hope it gives you some ideas and inspiration for what can be grown and, more importantly, what to do with the produce when harvested. After all, eating what you've grown is what it's all about.

Our black spaniel, Molly, stealing pears!

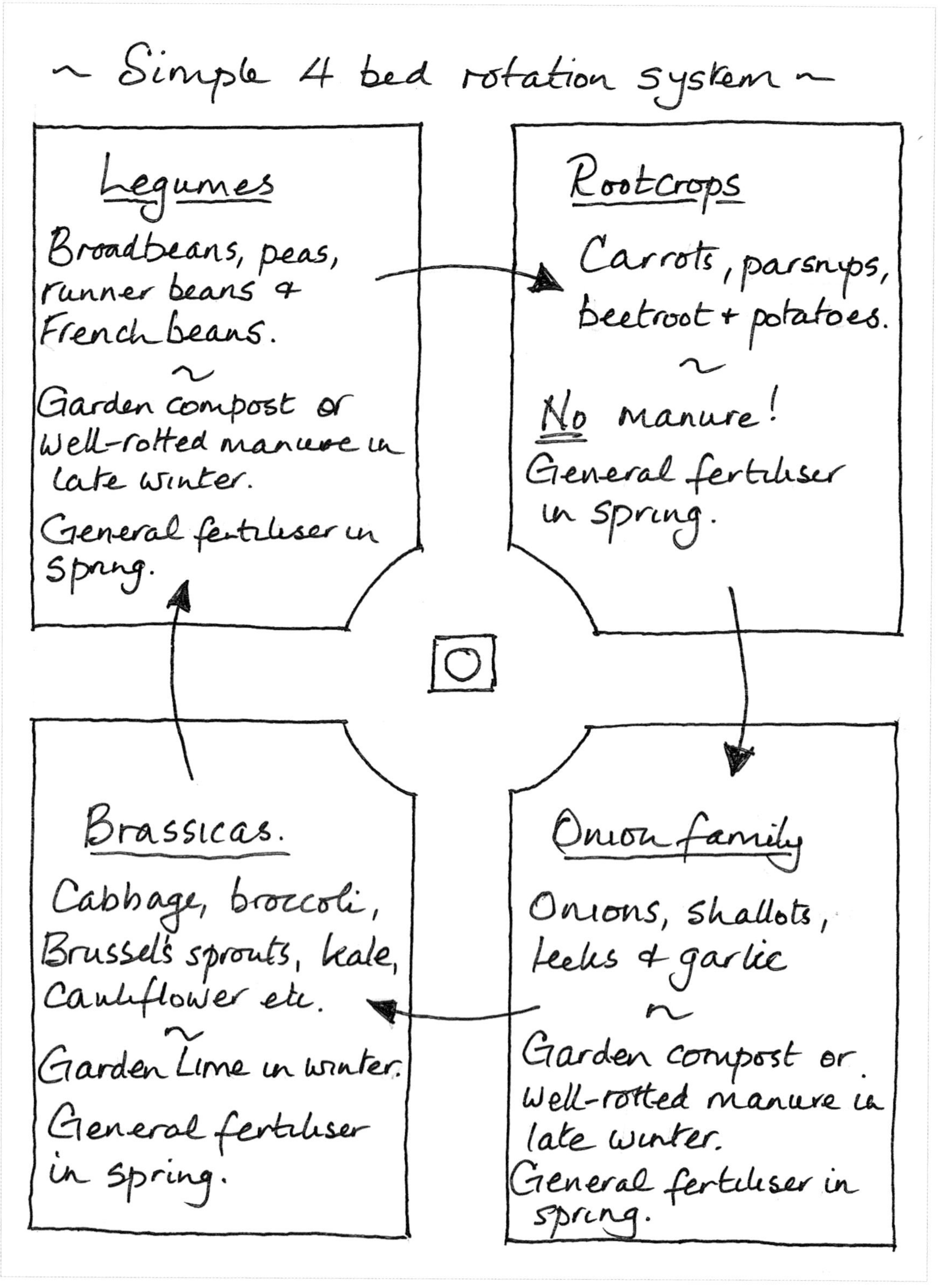

~ Simple 4 bed rotation system ~

Legumes

Broadbeans, peas, runner beans & French beans.

~

Garden compost or well-rotted manure in late winter.

General fertiliser in spring.

Rootcrops

Carrots, parsnips, beetroot + potatoes.

~

No manure!

General fertiliser in spring.

Onion family

Onions, shallots, leeks & garlic

~

Garden compost or well-rotted manure in late winter.

General fertiliser in spring.

Brassicas.

Cabbage, broccoli, Brussel's sprouts, kale, Cauliflower etc.

~

Garden Lime in winter.

General fertiliser in spring.

Using this book

Gardener's notes

Most growing references are based on the growing conditions in our North Yorkshire garden. We can get fairly cold winters and springs, hence the reason I like to start many vegetable plants off under cover to give them a head start. The bulk of seed sowing outside is done from early April onwards and tender vegetables are planted out around late May after the danger of frost has passed. Obviously, if you live further south, you can start a little earlier.

We grow on a simple rotation system of four beds that consist of legumes, root crops, onions and brassicas. The crops move clockwise around the plots, meaning they are only grown on the same soil every four years. This helps to keep the soil in good condition and prevents a build-up of pests and diseases. Vegetables such as salads and courgettes that don't fit into the rotation system are planted where there's a gap.

To improve the soil I use bulky organic matter in the form of home-made garden compost, well-rotted manure or spent mushroom compost from a local farm.

When I refer to using a general fertiliser, it is either Growmore, blood, fish and bone or dried poultry pellets. All supply a good balance of essential nutrients and I apply a couple of handfuls per square metre. I also often use sulphate of potash around fruit trees and bushes to supply potash which helps with flower and fruit development. We also use liquid feed for crops such as tomatoes, peppers and cucumbers through the summer.

Our soil is pH 7.0 which is neutral and fine for most vegetables. I do add garden lime to the brassica bed to raise the pH a little, which is what they like. If starting from scratch, I would advise you to carry out a simple soil pH test – kits only cost a couple of pounds.

The gardening side of this book is based very much on my experiences of growing fruit and vegetables over many years and even though I was trained in horticulture, I don't always get it right! Although I have mentioned a few common pests and diseases after each section, it's not a comprehensive list. I also haven't named any chemical treatments, simply because these are

From top to bottom: Martin getting the beds ready for spring planting and sowing, tying up bean poles and the vegetable plot at the height of the summer

changing all the time. For up-to-date information on pests and diseases and their control, the best place to look is on The Royal Horticultural Society's website - www.rhs.org.uk - which is updated on a regular basis.

Cook's notes

All these recipes have been used by our family for years, so rest assured that they are tried and tested!

I've included temperatures for conventional, fan and gas ovens. The timings are for conventional ovens, so if your fan oven cooks quickly then just check the timings every now and again.

Ingredients are listed as required. If the recipe calls for eggs, I usually use large.

- Teaspoons and tablespoons have been abbreviated to tsp and tblsp. I use measuring spoons that give 5ml for a teaspoon and 15ml for a tablespoon.
- I've only given metric measurements. I find I'm tempted to use a mixture of 'old' and 'new' if they're both there and that can be fatal - especially with baking!
- If a recipe needs some 'oil' then please use whatever you like. At the moment I'm using Yorkshire rapeseed oil for my cooking and I find it works well for everything - although I prefer extra virgin olive oil for salad dressings.
- I often say use a 'glug' or a 'good glug' of oil and a knob of butter - use your common sense and let it depend on the size of your pan and the quantities you're cooking. A glug would probably translate to a tablespoon and a knob is usually the size of a walnut.

Jam and chutney making

Pans - jam needs to be made in a wide, heavy-bottomed pan. It's worth investing in a jam pan (maslin pan) if you're going to be making bigger batches over the season as they have wide necks which allows jams to bubble up and gives chutney liquids room to evaporate.

Sterilising - all preserves need to be put into sterilised bottles or jars to ensure they last in storage without mould developing on the top - there's nothing worse than opening a jar of jam to find a layer of green mould growing there!

To ensure good sterilisation:

- Wash jars or bottles in hot soapy water and rinse clean
- Put upside down on a baking tray lined with a clean tea towel or kitchen roll
- Pop in a low oven – 140°C (fan 120°C), gas 1 – and leave to dry out completely for about 15 minutes
- Leave in a warm oven until ready to use

For the lids:

- Wash in hot soapy water and rinse clean
- Put in a bowl then cover with boiling water
- Leave for 3 or 4 minutes then drain and dry with kitchen roll
- Leave covered until ready to use

Vegetables

Asparagus in the garden

Asparagus is definitely one of our favourite vegetables and we look forward with anticipation each spring to the first tender spears that push through the soil. The taste of freshly cut spears sautéed in butter is wonderful and, as far as we are concerned, is far better than caviar or oysters!

Asparagus is definitely one vegetable we never eat out of season, simply because imported spears just do not taste as good as home grown. We eat it for around eight weeks a year which makes us appreciate it all the more!

Although not the easiest vegetable to grow, it's not the hardest and the effort that you have to put in to establishing and maintaining the plants is well worth it. Once established, asparagus should be productive for up to twenty years, but some people manage to keep it going much longer. When we started to create our new vegetable garden, asparagus was the very first thing we planted and the bed now provides us with tasty spears each year.

Soil conditions

To establish and grow well, asparagus needs good drainage and sandy soils are ideal. If it rains all day and night and you can still walk on the soil without it sticking to your boots too much, asparagus will grow. In wet, sticky clay soil the crowns will simply rot after a year or two or, at the very best, the plants will struggle and be weak! You can, of course, improve clay soils by working in plenty of bulky organic matter to help the drainage, but to stand a decent

Varieties

Although asparagus can be grown from seed, this extends the establishing time by another year, so most people buy one-year-old crowns. Modern cultivars tend to be all male, meaning the plants won't produce seed and you get stronger growth and thick spears.

In our garden we grow **'Backlim'**, which does very well.

'Backlim' – All-male hybrid that produces thick spears with purple tips.

'Gijnlim' – Another all-male type that produces succulent spears early in the season.

'Guelph Millennium' – A Canadian all-male variety that is ideal for UK growing conditions.

'Purple Pacific' – Produces thick, sweet-tasting purple spears.

chance of success it is worth creating ridges and planting on these so that surplus water can drain away from the roots. Alternatively, a raised bed filled with well-drained soil will do the trick.

The key to success is without doubt having a suitable soil and good soil preparation. Bearing in mind how long the plants are going to be in the ground, it pays to get it right from the start. First thing is to make sure all perennial weeds are controlled either by meticulously forking out the roots or by using a weedkiller that will kill the weed roots. The soil needs deep digging and organic matter should be worked in to create a deep root run for the asparagus.

Planting

Asparagus is usually sold as one-year-old plants called crowns. Occasionally you can buy them at nurseries or garden centres but they are mainly sold mail order by seed companies. Spring is the best time to plant, just as the soil is starting to warm up. The crowns should be dormant or just showing signs of the top bud coming to life. Dig out a trench in the newly prepared site approximately 30cm

Left, top: Mulching the bed in early spring.
Bottom: Planting asparagus crowns.

(12in) wide and 20cm (8in) deep, making sure the base is not compact. If you are planting more than one row, space the rows around 45cm (18in) apart. Using the spade, create a low ridge around 10cm (4in) high along the base of the trench and then place the crowns on the ridge 30cm–35cm (12in–14in) apart. When in position, the long fleshy roots should be straddling the ridge with the growth buds at the top. Backfill with fine soil and gently firm the soil around the roots. When planted, the tips of the crowns should be a couple of inches below the surface.

Aftercare

Shortly after planting, thin shoots will start to appear through the soil but under no circumstances should you cut any of the new shoots. For the first two growing seasons, allow all the shoots to develop into tall, ferny stalks. In hot, dry weather, make sure new plants are watered and you can also apply a liquid feed. A tomato fertiliser is ideal for this. If the tall stems start to topple over, it's a good idea to support them with strings or twiggy branches. At the end of the season the foliage will turn yellow in autumn and once it starts to naturally die down, cut it down to just above ground level.

In early spring, before there is any sign of growth, hand weed along the rows and very lightly fork between rows to tickle the surface of the soil and then sprinkle along some general fertiliser. In the past, gardeners would sprinkle salt along the rows because asparagus is a maritime plant, but it isn't necessary and if you over-do the salt, it can damage the roots.

After fertilising, I like to apply a mulch of around 5cm (2in) of well-rotted manure or garden compost.

Martin's tip

Always hand weed the asparagus bed because if you start hoeing between the plants to kill the weeds, you may damage the shallow roots and new shoots.

Harvesting

Traditionally asparagus is harvested between St George's Day, 23rd April, and the longest day, 21st June, giving around eight weeks of delicious asparagus. The exact timing does, however, depend on the season and where you live. In North Yorkshire it is often towards the end of April when we start cutting, but in the south the season can be a couple of weeks earlier.

Harvesting should start two years after planting, although the year after planting you can cut one spear per plant, but no more than that! From year two onwards, when the crowns are established, you can harvest all the spears when they are approximately 12.5cm (5in) tall. Use a long knife and push it down into the soil a short way to cut through the stalk. As the weather warms up into May, the spears grow very fast and you may need to cut two or three times a week.

At the end of the season (21st June), you have to be disciplined and stop cutting. This is to allow the spears to grow and develop into tall, ferny foliage over the summer which will help the plants build up strength for next year. I also like to give a feed with a general fertiliser in mid-summer to keep the plants growing and healthy.

Pests and diseases

Slugs and snails - They also like asparagus and if not controlled, will nibble the spears as they start to push through the soil.

Asparagus beetle - An increasing problem over recent years in some parts of the country is asparagus beetle. Both the adults and grubs feed on the foliage, causing defoliation through the summer. The beetles are black with a red thorax and yellow spots on the wing cases. Hand picking on a regular basis will help and in autumn burn the old stems when you cut them down to kill over-wintering beetles. Organic insecticides can also be used to kill the grubs.

Fungal diseases – Soil-borne diseases such as violet root rot, fusarium and foot rots can sometimes be a problem. The plants may be stunted, the new growth weak and pale or, in severe cases, the plant will collapse. These tend to be worse on wet, acid soils and on weak plants, so growing in the correct conditions and keeping plants well fed will help, as there are no treatments available.

Cutting down the ferny foliage in autumn when the stems turn yellow.

A favourite of Martin's - asparagus spears as soldiers to dunk in a boiled (or poached) egg!

Asparagus in the kitchen

Yum yum yum! We've been so lucky to be able to grow our own asparagus over the last few years. I'm afraid to say I have turned into an asparagus snob and I refuse to buy it from a supermarket now as it's just nowhere near as good as freshly picked! Fortunately, Maggie and James, some good friends in the village, farm asparagus so if our patch doesn't produce enough, then I pop in there where there's always some extra to buy in season.

When it's fresh from the garden it takes hardly any time to cook, maybe just two or three minutes. I simmer my stems in my deep-sided frying pan – no need for fancy steamers! Test by piercing the ends with a sharp knife. Whilst they're draining I melt a bit of butter in the pan then toss the spears in it along with some salt and pepper. Serve with some crusty granary bread and maybe a dash of balsamic vinegar and a few shavings of Parmesan cheese along with the buttery juices from the pan.

Enjoy asparagus on toast with shavings of parmesan and a dash of balsamic.

Rapeseed
Oil

Asparagus and Camembert tarts

This tart is ideal for a glut if you're lucky enough to have one and is great served cold for a picnic treat.

Makes 6 tarts

Takes about 25 minutes

Ingredients

- 1 sheet ready-rolled puff pastry
- 1 egg, beaten
- 12 asparagus spears
- Glug of oil
- Squeeze of lemon juice
- 6 slices Parma ham
- 175g Camembert or Brie, cut into small pieces
- 6 cherry tomatoes, halved
- Salt and pepper

Method

› Snap off the woody bottom part of the asparagus stem and discard (see Jill's tip on page 11). Cut off and keep the head of each spear. Bring a shallow pan of water to the boil and add the headless spears. Simmer gently for just 2 or 3 minutes depending on their thickness. Add the heads to blanch for just the last 45 seconds.

› Drain then return to the pan and toss in the oil and lemon juice and add a good grinding of salt and pepper. Leave to cool.

› Lay the slices of Parma ham on a board and cut in half lengthways. Wrap each asparagus spear in the ham.

› Unwrap and unroll the pastry. Leave on the plastic sheet and divide into 6 rectangles.

› Lay on a well-greased baking tray. Using a sharp knife, score a line around each side of each rectangle about 1cm away from the edge.

› Prick all over the inside of the scored rectangle with a fork then brush the whole rectangle with beaten egg.

› Lay 2 asparagus rolls and 2 asparagus heads on each rectangle then pop a couple of cherry tomato halves on each tart as well. Dot evenly with the Camembert (or Brie) pieces and sprinkle with salt and pepper.

› Pop in the oven, 200°C (fan 180°C) gas 6, for about 15–20 minutes until the pastry is golden brown and has risen round the edges and the cheese is bubbling hot.

Serve at once or eat at room temperature.

Warm new potato and asparagus salad

This is a really quick and easy recipe to do but is so tasty and one of Martin's favourites.

It is ideal for a light lunch or supper and is full of late spring flavour and colour. It's all about how the ingredients are put together and being ready to eat as soon as it's ready!

Serves 2

Takes about half an hour to prepare

Ingredients

1 red and 1 yellow skinned pepper, sliced
250g new potatoes, scrubbed clean
2 tblsps oil
½ tsp smoked paprika
About 10 asparagus spears, ends snapped off
5 cherry tomatoes, halved
2 large eggs
2 tblsps hollandaise sauce
Pan of hot water ready for poaching

Method

› Boil your new potatoes for about 10 minutes until just tender then drain and cut into thick slices.
› Mix 1 tablespoon of oil with the paprika in a large bowl then add the potato slices and coat well in the oil. Put to one side.
› Heat up a griddle or a frying pan. Brush the asparagus with some of the remaining oil and cook, turning once, for about 5–7 minutes, depending on how thick the spears are. Try not to move them too much as the charred stripes look really good in this dish. Transfer to a warm dish.
› Keep the griddle hot and add the potato slices. Cook for about 4 minutes until browning at the edges. Add to the asparagus and keep warm.
› Add the peppers and the tomatoes to the griddle (add a little more oil if necessary) and cook for just a couple of minutes to warm through, without the tomatoes losing their shape. Add to the potatoes and asparagus and toss very gently together. Plate up onto warmed, individual, shallow salad dishes.
› Poach the eggs in simmering water until the white is cooked but the yolk is still

runny. As soon as the egg is ready, lay carefully on top of the salad. Place a spoon of hollandaise sauce on top of the egg and finish with a good grinding of black pepper.

Eat immediately, letting the yolk run down onto the salad. Serve with some crusty bread to mop up the juices and yolk.

Jill's tip

Snap off the bottom part of the stem to get rid of the woody bottoms – you should be able to feel the resistance to know where to snap.

Easy no cook – Stir fry

Try slicing asparagus stems diagonally into 3cm-4cm sized pieces then stir fry in some oil. Add a few slices of garlic and some sliced or button mushrooms and cook until just tender. Splash on some light soy sauce or chicken stock then serve on a thick slice of toast.

Jill's tip

If you pick too many spears to use at once, pop the spare in a glass of water and cover the tops loosely with a small freezer bag and keep for a day or two in the fridge.

Beans in the garden

The legume plot in the garden is mainly taken up with beans of various types. We grow broad beans for an early summer crop which is then followed by traditional runner beans and dwarf French beans. What isn't eaten fresh from the plants is frozen for winter use. We also grow a few 'Borlotto' beans with their colourful seeds that are dried and used in stews and casseroles through the winter months. The plot more than provides us with enough beans for the year.

Broad beans

Broad beans are one of our favourite early summer vegetables, although I must admit as a child I didn't really like them very much at all. We always seemed to have them with gammon and the large, silvery beans always tasted bitter and they took some getting down!

Now, though, I can't get enough of them and when I'm out in the garden there is nothing nicer than popping open a pod to reveal tender green beans that taste delicious raw and cooked.

Growing broad beans is easy and a row in the garden will reward you with plenty of beans at a time when there's not that much fresh veg available in the garden.

Soil conditions

Broad beans will grow in most soils providing the roots are not waterlogged. I've grown them on clay soils and they have been fine, although for an early crop I find that lighter soils are best. Soil preparation is important and to grow well

Varieties

When choosing varieties, bear in mind that some will grow much taller than others. Catalogues have a good selection to choose from and it's worth trying a couple of different types.

'The Sutton' – A dwarf variety that grows to around 40cm (16in) tall and produces a good crop of pods.

'Aquadulce' – Traditionally sown in autumn. Grows to around 90cm (3ft) and produces long pods.

'Robin Hood' – Growing up in Sherwood Forest, I have to grow this one! A dwarf plant which only grows to 45cm (18in) with very tasty beans in June.

they like plenty of organic matter mixed into the soil. Dig garden compost or well-rotted manure into the ground in autumn or spring, depending on when you decide to plant.

'De Monica' – An early maturing variety and ideal for sowing in February. The plants grow to 90cm (3ft) and produce plenty of pods.

Sowing

Traditionally, many people used to sow the seed directly into the garden in autumn in the hope of getting an early crop the following June. However, in cold, wet winters the losses are high and the crop isn't much earlier!

Rather than subjecting the seedlings to being outside all winter, I much prefer to start the seed off under cover to produce strong, healthy seedlings for transplanting out into the garden when the soil conditions are better. I have sown in trays in November and kept the seedlings in a cold frame or polytunnel through the winter and then planted out in March, which has worked very well and given the plants a head start.

However, I mostly sow in early February when the days are getting longer and warmer and I find this way the seedlings grow much faster and catch up.

I sow in cell trays using multipurpose compost, with a single seed per cell. The seed will germinate at temperatures above 6°C, so even in a cold greenhouse they will soon start to grow. If you have some gentle heat in the greenhouse, all the better and you can sow a week or two earlier.

Planting and growing on

By mid-March you should have strong, sturdy seedlings that can be planted out into the garden. The plants are surprisingly tough and will withstand a little frost as long as they have been acclimatised to being outside for a couple of weeks before planting out. I plant with a trowel, spacing the plants approximately 20cm (8in) apart in all directions in a double or triple row, depending on how many plants I have.

Broad beans, like all legumes, fix nitrogen from the atmosphere onto root nodules which helps to feed the plant, but to give them a boost when they need to make growth in April and May, it's a good idea to feed, I simply sprinkle a little general fertiliser such as Growmore along the row and hoe it into the soil.

Keep the plants weed free and if you are growing the taller types, you

From top to bottom
Sowing seeds in cell trays which are germinated in the greenhouse or poly tunnel
Broad bean plants that have been hardened-off (acclimatised) in a cold frame
Planting out young plants in spring.

may need to erect some canes and string for support.

The attractive black and white flowers are produced up the stems (there is also a crimson flowering bean) and when they start to set and develop into beans, I pinch out the top few inches of the stems. This does two things: firstly, it diverts the plant's energy into the developing bean pods and, secondly, it helps to deter black bean aphid which can be a problem in the soft new growth.

Harvesting

If you want tender, green beans, pick the pods while they are still young, as and when you want a boiling. For a heavier yield you can let the beans grow on, but the larger beans are a little tougher, just like my childhood days! However, all is not lost as they can be double-podded, but I'll let Jill tell you all about that a little later.

If you intend to harvest in one go, it's much easier to cut the stalks off at ground level (see top photo on opposite page) with the bean pods attached and then do the picking sitting at a table.

Martin's tip

When you pinch out the growing tips, don't add them to the compost heap as they can be eaten. When cooked like spinach they have a lovely flavour and make a welcome addition to the dinner plate.

Pests and diseases

I find that plants sown in February or March grow faster and tend to be less prone to some of the problems from which beans can suffer, although they don't always escape. However, they are normally easy to grow, without too many problems.

Chocolate spot – This is easy to recognise as it shows as brown spots on the leaves and sometimes the pods. It's a fungal disease caused by a type of Botrytis and is usually worse on autumn-sown plants that have been stressed over winter. Avoid planting too close and encourage new spring growth by feeding. Badly affected plants which are starting to collapse need to be pulled out.

Bean aphid – (see image on right) The small blackflies feed by sucking sap from the plant and they tend to colonise in the growing tips where the growth is soft and juicy. Pinching off the growing tips after flowering helps. Alternatively, rub them off with your fingers, blast them off with a jet of water or use an approved insecticide.

Pea and bean weevil – The small beetles eat semicircular notches out of the leaves, but they don't really harm the plant too much. Feed in spring to encourage strong growth and plenty of foliage.

Mice – They can be a problem, especially where seed is sown directly into the garden. If they eat the seeds, set traps or consider starting the plants off in pots or trays under cover.

Martin's tip

All bean roots have nitrogen nodules attached to them. Don't dig them out; instead, leave the roots in the soil so that the nitrogen can help to feed the next crop, which on my rotation system is brassicas.

Runner beans

Probably still one of the most popular vegetables grown in vegetable gardens, simply because when freshly picked, they taste great. My dad wasn't much of a veg gardener, but he always liked to grow a few beans and like most people of my generation, I grew up with runner beans being one of the main summer vegetables on the Sunday lunch plate. We still look forward to the first runner beans of the season, which is usually in July.

Soil conditions

Runner beans are not too fussy about the soil as long as it retains moisture in the summer and contains plenty of organic matter. Preparing the soil where the beans are to be grown really does pay dividends. I usually work in plenty of garden compost or well-rotted manure in late winter in readiness.

What is important is the position, which needs to be in full sun and sheltered, as runner beans don't like a cold, windy spot.

Above: Decorative flowers of runner bean 'St George'.
Right: The resulting produce.

Martin's tip

To help seal in moisture around the runner bean roots in summer, give the soil a good soaking and then use fresh grass clippings as a thick mulch.

Top: Sowing runner beans in cell trays.
Left: A runner bean plant ready to start climbing.

Sowing

Just like broad beans, traditionally runner bean seed was sown directly into the garden in spring. However, if sown too early when the soil is cold and wet, the seed simply rots off. I now always start the seed off in cell trays of multipurpose compost in the greenhouse or polytunnel to produce plants ready for planting out when the danger of frost has passed.

Every year I get calls on the radio in April from people asking if they can plant out their bean plants which are a couple of feet tall! The answer is always no, because it's too cold. Runner beans are tender and will not stand any frost, so shouldn't be planted out until the danger of frost has passed, which for us in North Yorkshire is the end of May or early June, but I appreciate this will be earlier in the south. I, therefore, sow my seeds in the cell trays in early May and a month later I have plants at the perfect stage to plant out. You can also carry on sowing until June to get a later crop at the end of the summer.

Planting out and growing on

A week or so before planting, I apply some general fertiliser to the soil and work it in. The beans are planted out into the prepared soil when the weather conditions are right. Beans like plenty of water so if the soil is dry, give the roots a good soaking. The majority of runner beans grown in gardens are the climbing types and need support, although you can get dwarf varieties. I either plant up a wigwam of canes, usually eight plants in a 75cm (2ft 6in) circle,

Varieties

The catalogues are full of runner bean varieties and many of the more recent introductions have good resistance to diseases and are self-pollinating, helping to overcome problems with poor flower set.

Many also have bicoloured or different coloured flowers, making them very attractive in the veg plot.

'St George' – I've grown this one for a few years and it has always produced a heavy crop of beans. It also looks good with its red and white flowers.

'Firestorm' – I've also tried this one and again it did very well, producing a heavy crop. It has red flowers and is self-pollinating.

'Enorma' – As its name suggests, it produces long pods that not only taste good, they are also ideal for the show bench.

'Painted Lady' – This variety has been around for a few hundred years, but is still worth growing for its bicoloured flowers and small, tender beans.

The legume plot with broad beans, runners and dwarf French beans.

with the canes tied together at the top, or a single or double row of canes or hazel sticks. It doesn't really matter which you use as long as it supports the weight of the plants.

As the bean grows it will naturally twine around the support, although occasionally you need to point the bean at the cane! If you do need to give a helping hand, remember they twist around anti-clockwise (when viewed from above).

Through the summer, make sure the plants are kept well-watered, especially in dry weather, and when the plants get to the top of the canes, pinch out the growing tips to encourage side shoots and flowers.

Martin's tip

In hot, dry weather, mist the plants over at night with clear water to create humidity, which will help the flowers to set.

Harvesting

The secret with runner beans is to pick them while they are still tender and before seeds start to develop inside the pod. This may mean picking over the plants a couple of times a week through the main growing season. If you allow the beans to develop seeds and get large, the plants will naturally stop flowering, simply because they think they've done their job of producing seeds. Even if you can't eat them fast enough, pick them and freeze them or give them away. By picking little and often and with regular watering, you should be able to keep your beans fruiting until well into September.

'Hestia' – A dwarf bean that doesn't need any support that can be grown in the garden or in large containers.

Pests and diseases

Slugs and snails – Seedlings are prone to attack and if these pests aren't controlled, the plants will be eaten to ground level. Use organic pellets, beer traps, nematodes or whatever you usually use to control them.

Black bean aphid – This is usually a problem from mid-summer onwards. Squash the aphids when spotted, wash off with water or use an insecticide.

Root rots – This usually occurs when the plants are being grown in cold, wet, badly drained soils. Don't plant too early and make sure the soil is well prepared in advance.

No pods – This can be caused by poor flower set as a result of cold nights when the flowers open or hot, dry days. Keep the plants well-watered, mulched and fed, and mist the flowers at night. Modern varieties tend to suffer less. It can also be caused by sparrows that peck the flowers, so keep an eye out for them.

Top: Speckled borlotto beans for drying.
Bottom: Planting out dwarf French beans in late spring.

French beans

Another summer favourite that also freezes very well. There are various types of French beans, some are dwarf growing and others climb, just like runner beans. The shape of the bean also varies from flat pods to round, like a pencil, and they come in green, yellow and purple. Some types are also labelled Kenya beans, but they are all basically French beans.

In our garden we only grow dwarf French beans that grow no taller than 45cm (18in) and need no support. They are very productive and produce masses of very tasty beans from mid-summer onwards.

Sowing and growing

If you can grow runner beans, you can grow French beans - I basically treat them the same.

Although the seeds can be sown directly into the garden from late April, I prefer to start them in cell trays in the polytunnel. This way I don't have to worry about seeds rotting or seedlings being nibbled by slugs and snails. Growing in cell trays also means I can grow the exact number of plants that I want as when raised under cover, germination is very high. I sow the seeds in mid to late April to produce bushy plants for the garden at the end of May. When planted out, I space the plants approximately 20cm (8in) apart in all directions.

For an early crop, I also sow a small early batch in the heated greenhouse in March and these plants are then planted in the polytunnel border where they are protected from frost. These plants produce small, tender beans in early June.

Varieties

Because of the wide variety of French beans, seed catalogues always have a good selection to choose from. We now only grow the dwarf types, although in the past I've grown climbing varieties.

'Ferrari' – Often sold as a Kenya bean, this is a good, reliable bean to grow which I've grown several times. It's a short, compact plant with a heavy crop of pencil beans. It also has very good resistance to diseases.

'Purple Teepee' – Another dwarf variety that produces very compact plants and purple beans that turn green when cooked.

Harvesting

Like all beans, the sooner you pick, the more tender the beans will be. The dwarf types produce compact plants and the beans hang in clusters, so you may need to search for them amongst the foliage. They also have a shorter flowering period, meaning you tend to get the bulk of the beans all at once.

The exception, of course, is beans that are being grown for drying. These should be left on the plants until the pods have turned brown and the beans inside are loose when the pod is shaken.

Martin's tip

For a picking of fresh beans in September, sow a batch of seeds in June.

'Duel' – Fast maturing, dwarf, heavy cropping bean that produces its pods in clusters above the foliage, making them easy to pick.

'Hunter' – A climbing French bean that produces flat pods that are ideal for slicing.

'Borlotto Lingua di Fucco Nano' – This dwarf bean is an Italian speciality that produces green pods splashed with red. It can be eaten fresh or the beans can be dried and stored for winter use.

Pests and diseases

See the earlier section for runner beans.

Below: Freshly picked French beans.

Beans in the kitchen

Broad beans

Broad beans have a fairly short season so we try to make the most of them. They have different phases, though, and need to be treated differently according to how big the beans are.

The smallest beans are the simplest - just pod, boil for two to three minutes then drain, stir in some melted butter, season with a little salt and pepper and a squeeze of lemon juice and serve with some cooked meat or toss into salads.

Double podding

As they get bigger, the silvery skins become tougher and a little bitter so, although it takes time, it is worth taking off the skins. I call this double podding. It's really easy - after you've taken the beans out of their hairy outer pod, just pop in boiling water for a couple of minutes, then plunge in cold water and drain. Then I sit with the radio on and pop them out of their skins - it can be quite satisfying and a bowlful of the beautifully luscious, green beans that are exposed is a sight to behold!

Easy cook - purée

I often make a purée from them which is excellent used as a dip or a spread and freezes really well. Simply simmer until tender, drain (saving the cooking water) and after double podding, pop in a blender along with salt and pepper, a crushed garlic clove, plenty of fresh mint leaves and a good squeeze of lemon. Add a little of the cooking water and blitz. Add more water if necessary to make it the right thickness for spreading. Add a good dash of olive oil to make it silky smooth. Try adding a sprinkle of turmeric or a scattering of mint and serve with vegetable sticks. Or pop some on top of some bruschetta and add a topping of some ricotta cheese.

Broad bean and pea tabbouleh

Tabbouleh is a traditional middle eastern salad dish served with vegetables and herbs with a dressing of olive oil and lemon juice. Any fresh summer veg can be used along with broad beans and the herbs can be changed according to taste. Bulgur wheat is great in this dish - it has a light, nutty flavour and as we're trying to eat more wholegrain food, is a perfect swap for white rice. You could use couscous or brown rice.

Serves 4-6 as a side salad

Takes about 20 minutes to prepare

Ingredients

200g bulgur cracked wheat
600ml water
150g podded broad beans
75g baby peas
5 large spring onions, thinly sliced
Handful mangetout, chopped, or some chopped baby courgette
About 10 cherry tomatoes, halved
1 small lemon, zest and juice
½ red pepper, chopped
1 tblsp each of chopped parlsey, mint or basil and chives, chopped
Handful of watercress

For the dressing:

3 tblsps extra virgin olive oil

1 tblsp red wine vinegar

1 tblsp Dijon mustard

1 good tsp runny honey

Salt and pepper

Opposite, top: Double podding broad beans.
Bottom: Broad bean and pea tabbouleh.

Method

- Put the bulgur wheat in a saucepan with the water and bring to a boil. Simmer for about 10 minutes until the water is absorbed and the wheat is cooked through. Put to one side to cool. If the water hasn't been absorbed but the wheat is tender, then leave to drain for several minutes.
- Whilst the wheat is cooking, boil the broad beans for a couple of minutes then add the peas and cook for another minute. Drain and plunge into cold water. Drain again. Pick out any of the larger broad beans and slip off their skins.
- Use a fork to fluff up the bulgur wheat and put in a large mixing bowl. Scatter in the spring onions, lemon zest and juice and fork through, then add the broad beans and baby peas. Fork through gently then add in the tomatoes, mangetout and pepper.
- Scatter over the mixed, chopped herbs and a good grinding of salt and pepper.
- To make the honey and mustard dressing, mix all the ingredients in a small bowl, adding more honey if you like a sweeter taste.
- Pour three quarters of the dressing over the tabbouleh and mix well but gently using 2 wooden spoons. Add the remaining dressing if required. If you're making this ahead of time, cover and leave in the fridge.
- Pile into a large serving dish and tuck the watercress around the edges.

This is great as part of a summer buffet alongside quiche and cold meats or I serve on its own with cold meats and homemade pickles and chutneys.

> **Jill's tip**
> I like to use them as an ingredient in salad dishes as well, as when they are small we eat them raw, or just blanched.

Quick cook - risotto

Broad beans are a perfect addition to a risotto, along with a good squeeze of lemon juice, some mint and Parmesan cheese. You can also use them in a simple pasta dish with onions, lardons and crème fraiche.

Quick cook – Minty broad beans with crispy bacon

This is full of spring flavours and is really quick and easy to put together - a perfect lunchtime treat straight from the veg plot. If you've got leftover beans and potatoes from yesterday's meal, then this is a great way to use them up.

Serves 2 for lunch.

Only takes 10 minutes

Ingredients

8-10 small new potatoes, cooked and cooled
2 good handfuls each of baby broad beans and baby mangetout or peas, all just cooked and cooled
150g thin-cut streaky bacon or lardons
3 tblsps olive oil
Juice of ½ lemon
Black pepper
Good handful of mint, chopped

Method

- Heat your frying pan then add the bacon and fry until crispy and brown. Tip into a large bowl along with any cooking oil.
- Cut the potatoes into bite-size chunks and add to the bowl, stirring well to pick up the hot oil.
- In a small bowl, mix the lemon juice with the olive oil, a good grinding of black pepper and three quarters of the mint, and whisk well together.
- Put the beans and the mangetout into the bowl along with the bacon and potatoes, pour over the dressing and stir everything together.
- Scatter a little mint over the top and serve with some crusty bread to mop up the dressing.

Top: Adding herbs to broad bean tabboulah.
Centre: Omelette with broad bean shoots.
Bottom: Spring lasagne with baby broad beans and asparagus.

Jill's tip

Don't forget the young, tender shoots of broad beans – they taste so delicate and fresh.

Add them into an omelette or some scrambled egg at the end of cooking and they'll bring a whole new taste sensation to your eggs!

Easy cook – Spring lasagne

The start of the broad bean season usually crosses over with the end of the asparagus picking season, so make the most of the combination.

I make a really simple spring lasagne with asparagus and baby broad beans. I boil the veg until just tender then I make a sauce from some fried shallots, a squeeze of lemon juice, plenty of herbs (probably a mix of basil, mint and chives) and a good dollop or two of mascarpone. Simply sandwich the veg with half the sauce in between some cooked lasagne sheets then top with the other half of the sauce. Grate over plenty of Parmesan and serve straight away - perfect with a glass of something light and sparkly!

French and runner beans

The secret is to pick little and often whilst the beans are young, crisp and tender - easier said than done, I know - but it's really worth it as the taste is so much better than stringy, leathery beans. I'm getting a bit ruthless now that there's only the two of us and if they're too big, then they don't even make it to the kitchen; I bung them straight on the compost heap! Martin insists on growing two wigwams of runner beans every year which is always more than we need or can give away, so I can justify being picky about the ones that we eat and freeze.

Jill's tip

Preparing beans is less of a faff if you're using young veg as all you need to do is trim the tops and bottoms. If they are a bit older, then you may need to string runners – just run a potato peeler along the length to remove the tough outer sides of the bean. Slice runners thinly, diagonally across or lengthwise. Cut French beans into lengths as required.

Quick cook

Rather than a big recipe for French or runner beans, I thought I'd give you some quick ideas to try. Most of these work well with either variety.

It's easy to add some extra flavours to beans after cooking. Simmer or steam your beans until tender then add in some of these options:

- Fry shallots in butter then stir through cooked beans.
- Toss your beans in butter and some torn mint leaves - perfect for lamb - or try some tarragon in the butter.
- Melt some butter then add in some chopped hazelnuts and a squeeze of lemon juice. Add a little goat's cheese melted on the top for a dish on its own.
- Stir through some pesto for an extra kick.
- Add some sliced leeks whilst simmering beans, then whilst they're draining, fry some garlic in butter and add in some flaked almonds and a dash of soy sauce. Stir in the veg to coat - another good one for lamb.
- Cook your French beans with some baby carrots then toss in melted butter with some lemon zest and parsley thrown in.
- Try adding beans to a curry or stir them into some tomato sauce with a bit of extra chilli.

Quick cook – Bean and beetroot salad

Of course, beans can be eaten cold too - make sure they're young and fresh, though.

This is a great salad dish that can be knocked up in minutes and made ahead for the flavours to develop.

Serves 2

Takes 10 minutes to prepare

Ingredients

About 100g French or runner beans
About 100g cooked beetroot, cut into small cubes
Salad dressing made from 3 tblsps olive oil, ½ tblsp red wine vinegar and ½ tblsp balsamic vinegar (or use a ready-made balsamic dressing)
75g crumbly goat's cheese

Method

- Slice runner beans or halve French beans then simmer until just tender. Drain then rinse in cold water and drain again.
- Pop in a large bowl and add in the beetroot.
- Pour over your dressing then toss together.
- Crumble over the goat's cheese.

Jill's tips on freezing beans

Broad beans - Double pod your beans, then lay in a single layer on a tray lined with greaseproof paper and open freeze, packing them into a bag and sealing once they are solid.

French and runner beans - I always freeze enough to last us the winter and both types freeze really well. I don't bother blanching them first but if I've got a lot in one go, then I try and lay them in a flat layer in a large freezer bag then gather up the opening and suck out the air with a straw. This means that they don't freeze together in a clump, making it easy to get out a small amount.

Beetroot in the garden

Beetroot is a traditional summer vegetable for the garden, but its uses are often underestimated. As a child I only remember eating beetroot pickled in vinegar and you would have it with a salad or maybe cold meats. Although I love pickled beetroot, it can be cooked in so many ways and it is lovely when eaten warm as a vegetable.

However, my guilty pleasure in the summer is to pick fresh beetroot from the garden, boil it and when cooled, slice it. I then make a sandwich on white bread and add a good dollop of salad cream! Delicious, although not very inventive on the culinary front!

When you think of growing beetroot, don't just think of the traditional red, globe types as there are many others to choose from. They all taste great and have subtle differences.

As a crop in the garden, it is fairly easy to grow. It's not hardy, so the roots have to be lifted before winter sets in, but they can be stored to provide you with tasty beetroot for cooking or preserving right through the winter.

Soil conditions

Beetroot aren't that fussy really and will happily grow in most garden soils. I've grown them in heavy clay and light sandy soil and in both situations they have done well. Of course, the soil needs to be prepared in advance and with clay soils it helps if the ground has been previously manured or composted to help drainage. Don't, however, add fresh manure where you intend to grow beetroot or other root crops as it causes the roots to fork. As long as the soil is reasonably well drained and retains some moisture in the summer, they should be fine.

Varieties

Beetroot come in all shapes, sizes and colours, so if you have room in the garden, it's well worth trying some different varieties.

'Boltardy' – An old variety that is bolt-resistant and produces deep-red globe beet. A good all-rounder.

'Burpees Golden' – As its name suggests, it has golden flesh and a lovely, sweet flavour.

You can also grow beetroot in containers, especially if you only want small roots for summer salads. A multipurpose compost can be used, but I prefer to mix two parts multipurpose to one part loam-based compost to add a little weight and to retain moisture in dry weather.

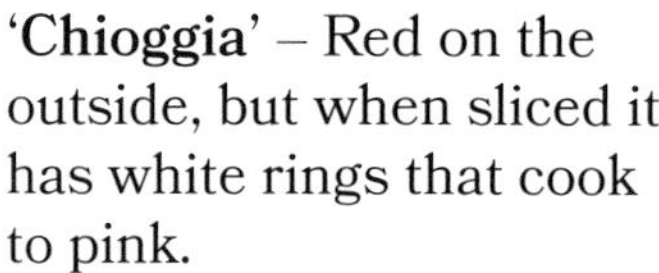
'Chioggia' – Red on the outside, but when sliced it has white rings that cook to pink.

'Alto' – A cylindrical type with long roots that grow out of the soil. Good flavour and keeps well. One of my favourites, especially for slicing on sandwiches.

'Moneta' – Produces one seedling per seed and is also bolt-resistant. Lovely, globe beets that are sweet when picked young.

Martin's tip

Crops sown early in the season have a tendency to run to seed so choose bolt-resistant varieties.

Beetroot varieties:
Top: The deep red globes of 'Boltardy'.
Centre: Sweet fleshed 'Burpees Golden'.
Bottom: 'Alto', with its long roots.

Sowing

Unless you live in a very mild area, there is no point sowing too early in the spring as the seeds won't germinate in cold, wet soil. I usually make the first outdoor sowing in early April when the soil is warming up. In the polytunnel where the soil warms up faster, I do make an early sowing at the beginning of March and cover the seeds over with fleece for extra protection.

The seeds are easy to handle and are sown in a shallow drill approximately 2.5cm (1in) deep. With most types of beetroot, what looks like a single large seed is actually a cluster of several seeds. Some varieties such as 'Moneta' are now sold as single seeds (monogerm) to save you having to thin the seedlings.

Sow the seeds thinly along the drill or, if you have the patience, space them around 3cm (1.5in) apart and carefully pull the soil over the seed row and gently tamp it down. Seedlings should start to emerge in around ten to fourteen days. For a continuous supply of small baby-beetroots through the summer and into autumn, sow a short row every two or three weeks from May to July.

Beetroot is one root vegetable that can be sown in plug trays or modules. This is a good way to start the seedlings off if you want an early crop or your soil is still too wet to sow directly into the garden. Sow a single seed cluster into a cell and germinate under cover. When the seedlings are still small, carefully remove without damaging the roots and plant out into the garden and water in. They normally grow away without any problems.

Aftercare

From each seed cluster, you should get two or three seedlings and when they are 2.5cm-5.0cm (1in-2in) tall you can thin them out to a single seedling. Ideally, each seedling should be around 7.5cm (3in) apart to give the roots space to develop over the coming weeks. The seedlings you pull out are great to mix in with leaf salads, so don't waste them!

Through the summer, keep the row watered in dry weather, especially when the roots are starting to swell and to prevent the plants running to seed (bolting). Of course, if weeds grow they will also need to be pulled out or hoed off.

Left: Sow beetroot seed in shallow drills.
Bottom: Thin seedlings when large enough to handle.

Harvesting and storing

You can pull the roots at any stage of growth and, of course, the young foliage can also be eaten in salads or cooked like spinach. When the roots are the size of a golf ball, they are very sweet and tender and are best pulled as needed. Roots that grow larger can be harvested in late summer and autumn and used fresh or stored for later use. The roots store well in a box or bucket of damp sand or compost if kept cool and frost-free. If they get too warm or dry, they will shrivel!

Pests and diseases

Although beetroot can be damaged by several pests and diseases, generally speaking they are not troubled too much.

Birds - Birds pecking at the small seedlings can be a problem which can easily be solved by draping some garden fleece over them.

Damping off - In wet weather, seedlings are prone to damping off, especially if sown too thickly. Try to avoid this by not sowing too close and thinning out the seedlings before they become crowded.

Leaf spot - Beetroot can also suffer from leaf spot, but this doesn't tend to bother the roots.

Martin's tip

When harvesting beetroot, never cut off the leaves as the roots will bleed sap. Instead, twist off the stalks just above the root.

Left: Twisting off the leaf stalks of freshly pulled roots.

Beetroot in the kitchen

I must admit that in the past I haven't always been a huge fan of beetroot. I think I was put off by eating limp slices of old, earthy beetroot pickled in strong vinegar at family teas!

Now though, I can pick beetroot straight from the plot while the roots are young and tender and I'll happily eat baby beets, which have a much milder flavour and can also be eaten raw. We like to grow the golden beetroot as well, which has a lovely gentle flavour and looks good in salads, plus it doesn't colour everything bright red!

As I've come to appreciate beetroot more, I've realised it's not just for pickling but can be used in loads of different ways in the kitchen.

Easy cook – Zesty Salad

Try grating beetroot and carrot together then toss in some orange juice and a bit of zest for a fresh, bright salad.

Beetroot and chocolate cake

This is a cake I often give to groups visiting the garden or when Martin and I do a 'Gardening on the Menu' talk - it never fails to get mixed reactions when the vegetable ingredient is revealed!

The beetroot gives it a rich ruby-red colour and keeps it really moist. It also helps it to last for several days. It's really easy to make.

Makes a 2lb loaf cake

Takes about an hour and a half

Ingredients

30g cocoa powder
180g plain flour
2 tsps baking powder
225g caster sugar
Pinch of salt
225g beetroot, boiled until tender
200ml corn or sunflower oil
1 tsp vanilla essence
3 eggs, beaten
100g plain chocolate, chopped small
A 2lb (900g) loaf tin, greased and lined

Method

› Sieve the flour, salt and cocoa powder together into a large bowl and stir in the sugar and chocolate.
› Peel the cold, boiled beetroot and grate finely or purée in a food processor. Put into a bowl and add the oil, eggs and vanilla essence. Beat together well.
› Make a well in the centre of the dry ingredients and pour in the beetroot mixture. Fold in slowly, making sure everything is incorporated but don't over-work the batter.
› Pour the batter into your prepared loaf tin and pop in the oven, 180°C (fan 160°C) gas 4, for about 1–1¼ hours.
› The cake is ready when a skewer comes out clean. If the top starts to burn, place a piece of tinfoil with a hole cut in the middle over the top of the cake.
› Leave to cool in the tin for 5 minutes then turn out onto a wire rack to cool.

Sprinkle with icing sugar and serve on its own or with a dollop of crème fraiche.

Beetroot chutney

Beetroot is perfect for making chutney and this one is quite tangy and refreshing. It goes well with just about any cheese or a good slice of ham.

Makes approximately 6 x 450g (1lb) jars

Ingredients

700g large beetroot
450g cooking apples
575ml vinegar
700g onions
450g granulated sugar
1 tsp salt
1-2 tsps ground ginger
½ tsp dried chilli flakes (optional)
Glass jars with vinegar-proof, screw-top lids

Method

Sterilise your jars according to the instructions in the Cook's notes in the Introduction to this book.

› Wash and trim your beetroot then pop into boiling water and cook until tender (half an hour to an hour, depending on their size). Testing is a bit like checking potatoes: a sharp knife will slide in easily when they're ready. Drain and leave to cool and store in the fridge if preparing ahead of time.
› Peel and chop the onions and apple into small chunks and put into a preserving pan along with half the vinegar. Bring to a gentle simmer and cook for about 10-15 minutes until the onion is tender.
› Peel and chop the beetroot into small chunks and add to the pan along with the rest of the vinegar, sugar, salt, ginger and chilli flakes, if using. Stir well to combine and dissolve the sugar and bring to the boil. Reduce the heat to a simmer. Stir often, making sure nothing catches on the bottom of the pan.
› The chutney is ready when it has thickened enough to be able to see the bottom of the pan on stirring. I like to test it by putting a spoonful on a chilled plate and running my finger through the middle of the chutney. If it leaves a clear path and you can see the plate, then your chutney is ready. It will thicken a bit more on cooling.
› Use a funnel and a small jug to pot up the chutney and seal with the lids immediately. Leave to cool then label and store in a cool, dark cupboard.

I know it's hard when you've made something fresh from the garden but this is really best if you leave the flavours to mature for six to eight weeks before eating.

Needless to say, we eat this with a large chunk of good, creamy Wensleydale and lots of crusty bread. Or try it on some toasted baguette topped with some runny goat's cheese - if you do it delicately, it would make a good nibble at a party!

Jill's tip - roasting beetroot

Have a go at roasting beetroot - the flavours become mellow and much sweeter. Try wrapping a couple of globes in a loose tinfoil parcel. For speed, just add in some oil and seasoning – thyme leaves work well – then roast for about an hour at 180°C (fan 160°C) gas 6, until tender. For added flavour, pop in a tablespoon each of olive oil, balsamic vinegar and redcurrant jelly along with the juice of half an orange before roasting.

Brassicas in the garden

The brassica family is very large and includes a wide variety of plants, including not only members of the cabbage family, but also many ornamental plants such as wallflowers and stocks.

In the vegetable garden, we tend to think of brassicas as cabbage, Brussels sprouts, kale, broccoli, cauliflower and calabrese, which are all leafy crops. By growing a selection of them it's possible to have some form of cabbage or brassica for twelve months of the year, making them an important part of the veg plot. Unfortunately, some brassicas have had bad press for many years and are the butt of jokes about school dinners and overcooked sprouts! But when cooked properly, they are all very tasty and nutritious vegetables and well worth growing. I like them all, but admit that for some, they are an acquired taste.

In this section I have concentrated on the selection of brassicas that we grow in our garden, which keep us supplied for most of the year.

Soil conditions

Ideally, brassicas like plenty of sun, although they will grow in partial shade. As for soil, they aren't too fussy and will grow perfectly well in light, sandy soil or heavy, clay soil and everything between. What they do require is a soil that retains moisture through the summer and a fair amount of nitrogen for all that leaf growth. On my rotation system, brassicas follow the legumes which have left behind nitrogen-fixing nodules on the old roots of peas and beans. The plot was also manured or composted for the legumes, leaving it in good condition for the cabbage family. Soil pH is also important and ideally should be pH 7.0 (neutral) or higher (alkaline) and to maintain these conditions I add garden lime to the plot at the start of the year. If you are not sure of the pH of your soil, it's well worth buying a simple kit for a few pounds to test it. I sprinkle a couple of handfuls of lime per square yard, but full instructions will be on the bag.

A couple of weeks before planting I apply a dressing of general fertiliser, rake it into the soil and tread the ground with my boots to firm it – vital for healthy growth.

Top: Liming the brassica plot to raise the pH.
Centre: Planting brassicas with a dibber.
Bottom: Fitting collars around cabbage.

Sowing and planting

Brassicas are all grown from seed sown at various times of the year. Summer cabbages and calabrese are sown in early spring to mature through the summer months. Winter cabbages, Brussels sprouts, kale and purple sprouting broccoli are sown in mid to late spring and harvested from October through the winter. Spring greens are sown in September and will be ready to harvest the following spring.

With all of them, I sow into cell trays of multipurpose compost. The seeds are large enough to handle individually and sowing this way allows you to grow the numbers needed for the plot. To germinate, the seeds do not need much heat and the polytunnel is fine. The seedlings grow on until they are around 10cm (4in) tall and have several leaves before being transplanted into the garden. When planting out, use a dibber or trowel and make sure the roots are well firmed into the soil.

Aftercare

If cabbage root fly is a problem in your garden, it pays to fit small collars around the base of the plants at planting time to prevent the flies laying eggs in the soil around the base of the plant. Pigeons can also be a serious problem and will destroy the young plants very quickly. To protect the plants, I cover them over with chicken wire made into low tunnels which allows me to check and water the plants for the first few weeks until they are established. When the plants start to push off the wire netting, it is replaced with a large, fine net to keep off butterflies, which are another problem. This physical barrier stops the butterflies laying eggs, but it needs to completely cover the crop to be effective.

Keep the plants weed free by hoeing between the rows and check for signs of pests and diseases.

Martin's tip

If removing the butterfly net to weed your cabbages, check that when it's replaced you haven't let in any butterflies!

Pests and diseases

All brassicas can suffer from the same problems, so I've listed a few of the main ones below.

Cabbage white butterflies – The white butterflies with dark markings on their wings are instantly recognisable. They lay their eggs on the underside of the leaves which hatch into caterpillars that eat very quickly. Ideally, cover with fine mesh to keep the butterflies off. If not covered, check for clumps of yellow–orange eggs or caterpillars and squash by hand or spray with an insecticide. Nematodes can also be used to help control the caterpillars.

Cabbage root fly – The adult root fly lays eggs in the soil at the base of the plant and the maggots that hatch eat the fibrous roots, causing the plant to look weak and eventually die. No insecticides are available, so fit collars if the pest is a problem or use nematodes.

Club root – This is a fungal disease that causes the roots of brassicas to swell and distort, leading to stunted plants and collapse. There are no treatments available and the spores can remain in the soil for many years – some say up to twenty! If club root is in your soil, raise plants and grow them on in pots to give them a head start when planted out. Also lime the plot heavily as the disease is less of a problem in alkaline soils. There are now also several varieties of cabbage, broccoli, calabrese, cauliflower and Brussels sprouts that have good resistance to the disease.

Mealy cabbage aphid – Greyish aphids colonise the underside of the leaves and cause leaf discolouration where they feed. If only a few, squash them, but where the infestation is heavy, use an insecticide.

Brassica whitefly – These are white-winged insects that feed on the underside of the leaves and fly when disturbed. Where they are in large numbers they can cause sooty mould to develop on the leaves. Control is difficult, and the whitefly don't appear to be harmed by sub-zero temperatures. Spraying with an insecticide will give some control.

Top: Insect proof mesh to keep butterflies at bay.
Bottom: Wire netting to protect young plants from pigeons.

Brussels sprouts

You either love them or hate them and in our house it's both! Jill hates them but I love them and will eat them cooked or raw when I'm working in the garden. Sprouts are a hardy winter vegetable that can be picked from early autumn through until spring. To ensure tight buttons on the stalks, make sure the plants are well firmed into the soil after planting. When grown in loosely cultivated soil, the sprouts often don't form properly and are not tight. As well as the sprouts, Brussel tops are also very tasty. This is the rosette of leaves at the top of the plant that is cooked like cabbage.

Varieties

Most varieties available are F1 hybrids that form compact plants, with some cropping early and others later in the season.

Seed is sown in March or April and the young plants are transplanted into the garden in May or June to grow on.

'Trafalgar' – Heavy crop of uniform sprouts that stand well through the winter months. Harvest from November to February.

'Crispus F1' – A mid-season variety that is resistant to club root. It produces dark-green sprouts from September to December.

'Rubine' – Purple sprouts that keep some of their colour when cooked. Harvest between November and February.

'Kalette Flower Sprout' – A cross between a Brussels sprout and kale. Produces very tasty, open, leafy sprouts with a mild, nutty flavour from October to March.

Kale

Probably the hardiest of all winter vegetables - it survived -19°C in our garden! It's also very nutritious and now classed as a 'superfood' and is one of my favourite winter vegetables. I've even been known to drink a kale and apple smoothie!

Some old varieties of kale are very tall growing, but the modern F1 hybrids tend to be more compact, making them suitable for small gardens. Kale is very easy to grow and the seeds are sown from March to May and planted out into the garden from late spring. Although eaten mainly as a winter vegetable, the young leaves can be pulled through the summer to extend the cropping season.

Varieties

'Curly Scarlet' – Deep-red curly leaves that get darker the colder it gets. The plants are totally hardy and leaves can be harvested between October and March.

'Nero di Toscana' – A variety of Italian black cabbage that is winter hardy and produces long, dark-green crinkly leaves from August through until March.

'Dwarf Green Curled' – Very hardy, green curly leaves on compact plants. Pull from September through to March.

Top: Kale 'Nero di Toscana'.
Bottom: Kale 'Curly Scarlet'.

Broccoli and calabrese

There's often confusion between broccoli and calabrese, but they are basically the same. Calabrese is usually harvested through the summer and broccoli is a winter and early spring veg. For summer and autumn, calabrese seeds can be sown in February, March or April and winter broccoli in April or May. Both types are grown in the garden exactly the same way, it's just that the summer varieties mature faster.

Both types are delicious and freeze well if you get a glut. Purple sprouting broccoli, which is harvested in spring, is always welcome as there aren't many fresh vegetables around at that time.

Varieties

Calabrese 'Marathon F1' – A reliable and long cropping variety that produces tight heads from July to November.

Calabrese 'Monclano F1' – A club root resistant variety that produces firm, domed heads from August to October.

Purple sprouting 'Claret F1' – Vigorous plants and a heavy crop of purple spears in March and April.

Purple sprouting 'Rudolph' – A long-cropping variety that produces purple spears from January to March, or even earlier if the seeds are sown early.

Above: Purple sprouting broccoli.
Left: Calabrese 'Marathon F1'.

Opposite page: Clearing the brassica plot in late spring.

Cabbage

It's possible to have cabbage fresh from the garden every month of the year. Some are large and round, others small and pointed, and it's surprising how the flavours differ. Seeds are sown at various times in order to get continuity and some varieties are much hardier than others, so if you want cabbages all year round, you need to do a little planning.

Spring cabbages ready to cut.

Varieties

Spring cabbage 'Durham Early' – Produces spring greens in late winter or can be left to mature to produce a pointed cabbage in April or May. Seeds are sown in July or August and planted out in October to overwinter.

Summer cabbage 'Sherwood F1' – Sow from February to June and harvest the solid, round heads from July to October. Has a sweet flavour and stands well in the garden.

Summer cabbage 'Caramba F1' – A very tasty, pointed sweetheart cabbage that is ready to harvest from July to September from an April sowing.

Autumn cabbage 'Kilaton F1' – A round, Dutch white type of cabbage with a solid head that is club root resistant. Sow in March or April and harvest from September to December.

Red cabbage 'Red Flare F1' – A medium-sized, round head, ideal for pickling or cooking. Sow in April and harvest between September and December.

Winter cabbage 'January King 3' (image on right) – An old, hardy variety that has red-tinged outer leaves. Sow in April and harvest from December through to March.

Winter cabbage 'Tundra F1' – A very hardy savoy cabbage with crinkly leaves that can be harvested from November to April from an April sowing.

Cauliflower

Cauliflower cheese takes me back to when I was a student at horticultural college. Through the winter, we had it once a week for an evening meal and I loved it!

With a little care and planning, it is possible to have fresh cauliflowers for many months of the year, but bear in mind that winter varieties produce large plants and are in the ground for almost a year! Cauliflowers do not like a check in growth, so plant out while the plants are still young and keep them watered until established.

Martin's tip

All brassicas benefit from a fertile soil, high in nitrogen. If growth looks slow in the summer, give the plants a couple of high-nitrogen liquid feeds a couple of weeks apart to boost their growth.

Varieties

'Clapton F1' – An autumn cropping cauliflower that produces a lovely white curd. Sow from March to May and harvest from September to November. It is also club root resistant.

'Mystique F1' – A vigorous, over-wintering type that is sown in April or May and produces white curds for cutting in February and March.

Brassicas in the kitchen

Cabbage, kale, sprouts, broccoli, to name just four

School dinners! How many of us were served boiled-to-death cabbage that made the school dining room smell for days? Any longer than a fifteen-minute boiling and sulphurous compounds are released to give that unmistakeable smell!

Fortunately it's not like that in schools and homes any more and we are all increasingly aware of the 'superfood' qualities of all of the brassica family. I'm not medically minded, but it's generally accepted that there are all sorts of health benefits from eating regular amounts of these vibrant green vegetables. Kale especially is known to be a medical powerhouse. I once read somewhere that eating regular amounts of kale was like having a tiny mechanic working constantly in our bodies, keeping our systems clean and functioning.

However, not all brassicas are particularly user friendly! When you're faced with a huge pile of leaves, it's sometimes hard to know what to do with them.

Jill's tips

- The one thing I'd say about all the brassica family is – don't overcook them. The longer they are cooked, the less health benefits they'll have as a lot of the nutrients will be boiled away.
- Balance out the strong taste with other flavours – cream, cheese, honey or balsamic vinegar will all level out any aggressive flavours. Or match the strong flavours with ingredients like chilli, pancetta, mustard or Parmesan.
- For simplicity, steam or simmer prepared brassicas until just tender, then drain and lightly toss in the pan with some oil, garlic and salt.
- If you want to store cooked brassicas, make sure they cool down completely before putting the lid on the container. Cooking damages the cell walls of the vegetable, which starts to release the sulphur compounds. If it's enclosed in an airtight container, the smell will only get worse!

I couldn't include a recipe for every member of the brassica family but these are some of our favourites. I hope they add a twist or two but still let the flavours flood through.

Purple sprouting broccoli

The trick to cooking purple sprouting broccoli is to cook it evenly – if the stems are quite thick, then cut them through lengthways first. This will ensure that the florets don't get soggy before the stalks are tender. Alternatively, cut the stems across diagonally in thick slices to cook.

In stir fries, smallish pieces of purple sprouting broccoli only take three or four minutes to cook and will simmer or steam in just five or six minutes. Toss in some oil and lemon juice after cooking or, for a treat, cook, then toss in butter and top with a lightly poached egg.

Purple sprouting broccoli on toast

Serves 2

Takes about 15 minutes

This is a quick, easy dish that can be served as a light lunch or supper. I use ciabatta bread for the toast as it's got a firm crusty base that holds in all the delicious juices!

Ingredients

Large knob of butter
2 glugs of oil
5 or 6 stalks purple sprouting broccoli, cut into smallish pieces
1 clove garlic, crushed
Approx 12 button mushrooms or 6 mushrooms, thickly sliced
Salt and pepper
1 small ciabatta loaf
150g Dolcelatte cheese (or a soft, creamy blue cheese)

Method

› Slice the ciabatta loaf in half lengthways and brush the top with a good glug of olive oil. Preheat the grill and pop the bread under. Grill on medium-high until lightly toasted on top. Turn and grill lightly underneath.
› Simmer the broccoli for about 3–4 minutes until only just tender. Drain and keep warm.
› Melt the butter in a frying pan and sauté the mushrooms. Add the garlic and season well with salt and pepper. Cook until the mushrooms start to release their garlicky juices then add in the purple sprouting broccoli and stir to reheat.
› Share the broccoli and mushrooms between the ciabatta toasts, piling the mixture fairly high. Pour over any juices left in the pan.
› Break up the Dolcelatte cheese into smallish pieces and place on top of the broccoli. Put under a medium-hot grill and heat until the cheese has melted and run down into the broccoli and mushrooms.

Serve immediately and for an extra tasty treat, pop some smoked bacon onto the top for an extra flavour. (See photo on p68.)

Kale

Sautéed, roasted, steamed or simmered, kale is quite a versatile vegetable with a unique earthy, minerally taste of its own but the most health benefits are believed to be in raw kale. Kale has certainly undergone a facelift in the last few years and supermarket fridges all contain fresh kale juice. Harriet, our youngest daughter, persuaded us to try kale juice last year - I think she's trying to keep the old folks fit and healthy!

Easy cook – Kale and leeks

Mix cooked kale with some buttery leeks for a tasty side dish. (See bottom photo on opposite page.)

Jill's tips - *see photos below*

- Remove the spines of kale before cutting - they can be tough and bitter to eat. Lay on a board, fold in half and simply cut them away.
- If you're eating kale raw in a salad, then it needs to be shredded - simply stack several leaves together and roll into a cigar shape then cut crosswise as thinly as possible.

Opposite page, top: Purple sprouting broccoli on toast.

Bottom: Mix kale and leeks with melted butter for a tasty combination.

Jill's tips - juicing

- Kale juice is easy to make at home if you've got a juicer, but add in some apples and ginger, or cucumber and mint, to make it go further and calm the taste down a little.
- If you've got a blender, then add in some liquid to cover your chopped kale – water, milk or maybe coconut water – and blitz until smooth. Add in some chopped fruit or some celery. Pass through a sieve if you want a smoother texture.

Caldo verde

For several years, Martin used to go off on a boys' holiday to Portugal for a few days. The gang of friends went to do some clay pigeon shooting but I suspect that once they'd shot a few rounds in the mornings, it was down to the bars for a few beers! On their return, some of the wives would get perfume or chocolates from the duty free but Martin, being Martin, used to bring back recipes from the places they'd had lunch! This traditional Portuguese dish is served in most of the local bars and will keep hunger pangs at bay for quite a time.

This is a thick, tasty soup that is filling enough on its own for a good lunch or supper. The kale is added in the last few minutes so it still retains a bite and all its healthy nature.

Serves 6

Takes about 30 minutes

Ingredients

2 tblsps olive oil
1 large onion, chopped
2 cloves garlic, crushed
4 large potatoes, peeled and diced
200g chorizo, sliced fairly thinly
1 litre vegetable stock
300g kale, stems removed and sliced thinly
Black pepper

For serving

Extra virgin olive oil
Good pinch of paprika

Method

› Heat the oil in a large pan and add the onions and garlic. Cook gently for about 5 minutes with the lid on until just softened but not browning.
› Add the chorizo slices and fry for just a few minutes to release some of its oils and flavours. Add the diced potato and stir to coat in the oil. Remove the chorizo and put on one side.
› Pour in the stock and bring to a simmer. Leave to cook for about 12-15 minutes until the potatoes are soft.
› Use a potato masher to gently break down the onions and potato until you have a thick, soupy consistency with some smallish lumps.
› Add the shredded kale to the pan along with the chorizo and heat through at a simmer for about 5 minutes.

To serve, pour some extra virgin olive oil into a small bowl and add a good pinch of paprika. Ladle some soup into deep bowls then swirl the oil over the top of the caldo verde.

Brussels sprouts

I'm not a big sprout fan – on Christmas Day Martin makes me have one on my plate but I always try to sneak it onto his when he's not looking! For this book I've had to face my demons and try some recipes with them and I have to say I was pleasantly surprised with this recipe. We had it for Christmas dinner this year and I actually went back for seconds!

Creamy sprouts

Serves 6

Takes about 15 minutes

Ingredients

600g Brussels sprouts, trimmed
1 large onion, finely chopped
Small glug of oil and small knob of butter for frying
15g butter
1 garlic clove, crushed
¼ vegetable or chicken stock cube
150ml double cream
2 good pinches of ground nutmeg
100g pine nuts

Method

› Pile the sprouts into a pan of boiling water and cook for 3–4 minutes until just tender. Drain and rinse immediately in cold water. Drain and set aside.
› Heat the oil and butter in a frying pan and fry the onions gently for about 10 minutes until softened but not coloured. Crumble in the stock cube and add the garlic and cook together for a couple of minutes. Turn the heat down low.
› Whilst the onions are cooking, chop the sprouts or slice them, then add into the onions along with the rest of the butter, the double cream and 1 pinch of nutmeg.
› Increase the heat slightly and bring to a gentle simmer to warm through and season to taste.
› Add in the pine nuts and serve with an extra sprinkling of nutmeg.

To get ahead, cook and slice the sprouts, cook the onions and mix together. When ready to serve, simply heat through and add the cream, nutmeg and pine nuts. This dish will stand being reheated – just microwave until hot throughout.

Jill's tip

Please don't forget the sprout tops – there's a little parcel of delight at the top of each stalk! A much milder flavour, more like cabbages with a hint of sprout and in a ready-to-eat serving.
They don't take much cooking: just slice and simmer for 5–6 minutes or steam for about 8 minutes. They stir fry well or could be added into soups and pasta sauces.

Easy cook – Stir fry

Quarter some baby sprouts and mix with some shredded curly kale. Stir fry some chicken then add in the veg until just cooked. Add in a splash of white wine vinegar and a good dash of soy sauce and the zest and juice of half a lime.

Easy cook – Spicy sprouts

Slice some sprouts and heat some oil (coconut is good with this dish) in a frying pan. Fry a scattering of cumin seeds for just 10 seconds to release the smell then add in the sliced sprouts. Stir constantly over quite a high heat until softened and browning in places. Sprinkle on some fresh-torn coriander or some desiccated coconut.

Cabbage

It's hard to believe how many types of cabbage there are and they cover all the year, from the early spring greens through to the hardy winter cabbages. I think my favourite is the sweetheart type - it has a gentle flavour and one will give us just enough for a couple of meals without any going to waste.

Remember, don't overcook your cabbage, whatever the variety - it should still have a bit of a bite to it. Always cut out the core of any cabbage before slicing and if you're eating it raw, make sure you shred it finely.

Easy cook – Smoky cabbage

Fry some lardons of smoky bacon and some onion, then add in some only-just-cooked cabbage. Toss to coat and absorb the flavours.

Or add this mix into some mashed potato for a version of colcannon. Add in a good measure of double cream and a knob of butter as well when mashing the potato, then stir through the cabbage mixture.

Winter coleslaw

Red cabbage is perfect for strong flavours as it's such a robust vegetable. It will stand being slow cooked or pickled but is good eaten raw as well. This winter coleslaw is perfect for a buffet - full of colour and wintery flavours.

Serves 6-8 people as a side dish but can easily be halved

Takes about 10 minutes plus an hour to stand

This is a low-fat version but you can, of course, use full-fat dressing ingredients!

Ingredients

½ small red cabbage
¼ small white cabbage
1 small red onion, finely sliced
1 red pepper, finely sliced
1 large carrot, peeled and grated
1 red eating apple
50g dried cranberries

For the dressing:

4 tblsps low-fat natural yoghurt
3 tblsps low-fat mayonnaise
2 tblsps cranberry sauce

Method

- Peel off the outer leaves of the cabbages then use a really sharp knife to shred them as finely as possible. It helps to cut the cabbage into quarters first. Put in a very large bowl.
- Add in the onion, pepper, carrot and dried cranberries and toss everything together.
- In a small bowl, mix together the dressing ingredients until creamy and smooth.
- Halve and core the apple, then chop fairly finely, leaving on the peel. Add to the cabbage bowl.
- Spoon in the dressing and carefully try to coat all the ingredients. At first it looks as if it won't be enough, but persevere!
- Pile into a serving bowl then cover and pop in the fridge for an hour to let the flavours mingle together.

This can be made a few hours ahead but is best eaten fresh as the coleslaw ingredients can become a little watery.

Courgettes and marrows in the garden

Essentially, courgettes and marrows are the same – we eat one when it is small and immature and the other when it has been allowed to develop to full size. As a child I remember seeing marrows growing in gardens, but courgettes didn't really feature! They were around, of course, but back in the old days we tended to call them 'baby' marrows. It was in the 1960s when people started to take more holidays abroad that they became a more popular part of our diet. In France they were known as courgettes and the Italians knew them as zucchini. Nowadays, courgettes are more widely grown than marrows and over recent years more and more varieties of courgette have been introduced into the gardening market. But beware, if they aren't picked when small and tender, they will turn into giant marrows!

Soil conditions

To grow well they need an open, sunny site and good fertile soil that has been prepared by adding in plenty of organic matter to help retain moisture and nutrients over the summer. Just before planting, I also sprinkle a few handfuls of general fertiliser over the area and lightly work it into the soil.

Sowing and planting

The seeds of courgettes and marrows can be sown directly outside in the garden in late spring, but slugs and snails love the new shoots, so I tend to start the plants off under cover.

I sow in cell trays of multipurpose compost and germinate them in the greenhouse in gentle heat of around 15°C. I do this around mid-April to produce plants for the garden at the end of May. When the danger of frost has passed, I plant

Varieties

You'll find a larger selection of courgettes than marrows in catalogues, but remember that courgettes develop into marrows and for that reason we only grow courgettes in our garden. Many varieties now have resistance to diseases and are bred for our cooler climate.

Top: Sowing courgette seeds in cell trays.
Above left: A male courgette flower.
Above right: A young courgette plant being planted out.

out into the prepared soil. As courgettes don't fit directly into our four-bed rotation system, I plant them where there's a large enough space between other veg. Plant approximately 90cm (36in) apart to give them room to develop.

Courgettes can also be grown in large pots of multipurpose compost and will produce a good crop of tender fruits. The plants will need plenty of water and a weekly liquid feed such as tomato fertiliser to keep them growing and healthy.

Martin's tip

For early courgettes, sow the seed in a heated greenhouse in March and grow the plants on in pots under cover to establish. When planted out, the larger plants will soon start to produce fruits

Aftercare

In dry weather the plants need to be watered to help them establish and weeds need to be controlled. It's also important to make sure they have plenty of water when they start to flower and produce fruits. If the plants seem to slow down a little, give a few liquid feeds as a boost.

They produce two types of flower: male and female. I remember my Grandma showing me how to pollinate the plants by removing the open male flower with a slender stalk and pushing it into the open female flower with the embryo fruit behind it, to transfer pollen. Insects and bees normally pollinate the flowers, but if it's cool or there aren't many flying insects around, it's worth pollinating by hand to ensure a good crop.

Courgette **'Defender'** – A good, reliable variety that produces early green fruits on plants with good disease resistance.

Courgette **'Atena Polka'** – A yellow variety that produces plenty of fruit and looks great on the plate.

Courgette **'Black Forest'** – A climbing variety with dark-green fruits. Ideal for growing in containers up a wigwam.

Courgette **'One Ball'** – Produces yellow, round fruits about the size of a tennis ball. Fun to grow and with the same courgette flavour. Best picked when young.

Marrow **'Tiger Cross'** – Early to mature, dark-green striped fruits that store well.

Harvesting

Courgettes are at their best when harvested between 10cm-15cm (4in-6in) long and should simply be cut off at the stalk with a sharp knife. Once they start to flower and produce fruits, check them at least twice a week as the fruits grow very quickly! If you go away on holiday in the summer, you'll come back to marrows!

As we only grow courgette varieties, we pick small fruits regularly and towards the end of the summer we allow some fruits to grow and mature into marrows. However, when you stop picking regularly, the plants stop flowering, so bear that in mind.

If growing marrow varieties, they can, of course, be picked when small as 'baby' marrows. If you want large marrows for use through the autumn or winter, allow them to mature on the plant.

Courgettes have soft skins and don't store for more than a few days in the fridge. Marrows, on the other hand, (including courgettes that have matured), will develop a hard skin in late summer and early autumn and will keep for a few months. To help the skin ripen (known as curing) allow maximum sunlight to the fruits, or when harvested, stand them out in a sunny position for a week or so to cure. The harder the skin, the longer they will keep in a dry, airy place.

Pests and diseases

Powdery mildew – Shows as a white substance on the leaf and is worse late in the season. Keep the plants watered and fed through the summer. Some varieties have very good resistance.

Mosaic virus – Results in mottled foliage and poorly formed fruits. No treatments are available, although resistant varieties are available.

Slugs and snails – Can cause damage to young plants and developing fruits. Control with beer traps, nematodes, pellets or a barrier.

Fruit rotting – Can be a problem in cool, damp weather. The old flower rots and spreads back into the fruit. Avoid watering over the foliage and flowers in cool weather and pick off and dispose of damaged fruits.

Martin's tip

Store ripe marrows in old tights or nets and hang them in a frost-free shed where they should keep until at least Christmas.

Right: Courgette fruit rot.
Below, top: Courgette '**Defender**' at the perfect size to harvest.
Bottom: Courgette '**Atena Polka**'.

Courgettes and marrows in the kitchen

Along with cucumbers, I think courgettes are the biggest 'glut' problem in the garden. Of course, we all know that we have to pick little and often to get the tastiest fruits, but sometimes it's hard to know what to do with them!

I tend to use them in everything and add them into pasta sauces, risottos and salads. I make chutney for the store cupboard and batches of soup and ratatouille for the freezer and courgette cake is delicious!

And, of course, you can never go away for even a day, as then you have to face marrows! We deliberately leave three or four courgettes at the end of the season so that I have some marrows for the kitchen. They are a bit of a blank canvas so can have all sorts of flavours added to them - rosemary, marjoram and chilli work well - and they can be stuffed with sauces or just cooked with cheese.

Jill's tip
Spiralisers are all the rage as we write this book and they are a great way to serve courgettes – simply stir fry or drop in boiling water for just a few seconds – use instead of spaghetti or noodles. If you haven't got a spiraliser, then use a vegetable peeler to slice thin ribbons or coarsely grate for more or less the same effect.

Opposite page: Marrows ripening before storing in a frost free shed.

Quick no cook – Creamy courgette salad

For a delicious light salad, bring out the flavour of your courgettes with some mint. Slice about 4 or 5 small courgettes into thin ribbons with a vegetable peeler or spiraliser. Thinly slice a red onion and squeeze over the juice of a lemon and leave to stand for a little while to soften. Tip into a large serving bowl with the courgette ribbons, add a good handful of chopped mint and spoon in about 4 tablespoons of mayonnaise. Toss everything together, trying not to break up the courgette ribbons.

Jill's tip - courgettes

As a side dish, I tend to sauté courgettes in a little butter in a frying pan until they are browning at the edges but lovely and soft inside. Depending on what I'm serving them with, I will add in a few herbs at the last minute of cooking. Thyme always works well with courgettes, especially when serving with fish or pork.

Courgette, ham and apple persillade

On one of our favourite French holidays, we had the most delicious warm salads made from courgettes and served with a persillade dressing. This is simpler than it sounds – it's just parsley and garlic mixed with a little oil.

Serves 4–6

Takes about 30 minutes

Ingredients

500g (about 6 small to medium-sized) courgettes
Table salt
1 red onion, peeled and thinly sliced
1 red pepper, chopped into small pieces
4 tblsps olive oil
1 dessert apple
2 tomatoes, chopped small
250g thick cooked ham (smoked is good), chopped into small bite-size pieces
Salt and pepper
Medium bunch parsley, finely chopped
2 cloves garlic, crushed
Good glug extra virgin olive oil

Method

- Cut the courgettes into thin batons then put into a large bowl and sprinkle over some salt. Toss together and leave for a few minutes, then rinse and pat dry.
- Heat half the oil in a large frying pan and fry the courgettes over a medium heat until they release their watery juices. Turn the heat up a bit and fry to evaporate the liquid and soften the courgettes without letting them brown too much. Put to one side.
- Heat the remaining 2 tablespoons of the oil in the large frying pan and add the onions and the pepper. Fry for about 7 minutes until just softening but not browning.
- Cut the apple into quarters, core and chop, leaving the peel on, and add to the pan along with the tomato and the ham. Cook over a low heat for about 4 minutes, stirring occasionally to prevent sticking. Don't let the apple get too soft at this stage.
- Return the courgettes to the pan and cook over a low heat for about 5 minutes until everything is nicely tender.

Make the persillade:

Put the parsley into a bowl then add the crushed garlic. Pour in just enough extra virgin olive oil to make a thick paste.

Tip this into the pan and stir well to coat everything in the herby mixture. Leave to cook for a few more minutes to cook the garlic a little, then grind over some black pepper and salt, if required.

Serve immediately, although it tastes good too when served at room temperature the next day.

Jill's tips - marrows

Size really does matter! I don't tend to use marrows if they are longer than Martin's forearm. They can get quite bitter and watery, so chop them up and let the compost heap benefit!

Roast marrow - You can try roasting marrow – cut it into large chunks and remove the peel and seeds. Butter an ovenproof dish then lay in the marrow chunks. Scatter over plenty of marjoram and pepper then add a sprinkling of sugar and some dots of butter. Cover with foil and bake for about 30 minutes at 160°C(140°C fan), gas 3. Remove the foil and pop back in for another 15 minutes until soft and tender.

Marrow and ginger jam

My Dad's favourite treat was always ice cream with Mum's marrow and ginger jam. She made it every year and he loved it. I have to say I wasn't a fan when I was little - I think her cubes of marrow were too big for me - but I started to make it a few years ago from her recipe and we all love it. In fact Richard, our youngest, always gets a jar in his Christmas stocking!

Makes about 6 x 370ml (1lb) jars

Takes about an hour plus chopping and resting overnight

Ingredients and equipment

- 1.3kg marrow flesh, seeds and any fibrous strands removed
- 1.6kg granulated sugar
- 30g root ginger, cut into chunks and crushed
- 2 large lemons and 1 orange
- 5 or 6 balls of stem ginger, diced (optional)
- Sterilised jam jars & lids
- Muslin to make a small bag
- Saucer in the freezer for testing the setting point

Method

- Peel and dice the marrow into evenly sized, small (up to 1cm) cubes. Put into a large basin with half the sugar. Stir well, cover and leave overnight. It will produce quite a lot of syrup, so don't worry!
- Squeeze the juice from the fruits and reserve, then chop up the peel and flesh.
- Place the ginger and peel in the muslin and make it into a secure bag.
- Pour all the marrow and syrup into your preserving pan then add the muslin bag along with the juice from the fruits.
- Stir on a low heat until the sugar is dissolved then increase the heat to a simmer for 30 minutes.
- Lower the heat and add the rest of the sugar and stir until it's completely dissolved.
- Boil gently for approx 15–20 minutes until the marrow has become transparent and setting point is reached. Turn the heat off and put a teaspoon full of jam on your frozen saucer. Leave for a minute then run your finger through it. You're looking for a soft set with this jam so if there's a little wrinkle, it's ready. If not, pop back on the heat and boil for another 2 minutes and test again.
- Take out the muslin bag and squeeze really well to release any juices.
- Add the diced stem ginger, if using, and stir in well.
- Leave to cool slightly, then pour carefully into warm jars and cover with screw-top lids.
- Cool then store in a cool dark place. Once opened, it will keep in the fridge for several weeks.

Like Dad, we use this mainly as a topping for vanilla ice cream but it's delicious on the top of a baked apple. You could also try serving this with a sponge pudding or even a Yorkshire pud left over from the Sunday roast!

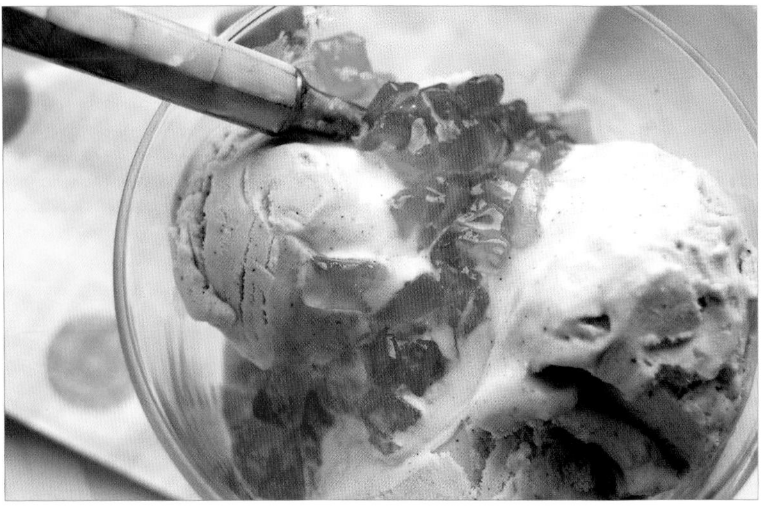

Cucumbers in the garden

A fresh cucumber picked from the greenhouse tastes wonderful and much better than one bought from a shop. Cucumbers do require a little bit of cossetting, but they are well worth it.

There are different types of cucumber suitable for growing under cover or outdoors in warm areas, but I only grow the greenhouse types. I have, however, grown gherkins in the past in the polytunnel and pickled the fruits, which are delicious. I always think that when we start to pick cucumbers, summer is well and truly here!

Growing and soil conditions

Warmth, especially when the plants are young and establishing, is essential. If you are growing in an unheated greenhouse or polytunnel, I wouldn't consider planting out young plants until well into May. If planted in cool conditions, they struggle and often die, whereas when planted in warm soil they romp away!

They are greedy feeders and traditionally were grown on hotbeds prepared with manure to generate heat and fed with dried blood to supply nitrogen during the early stages of growth.

If growing them in a greenhouse border, improve the soil by working in plenty of well-rotted manure or garden compost which will help to retain moisture in summer. You need to feed the soil with a general fertiliser and I tend to use dried poultry pellets as they have a slightly higher nitrogen content.

Alternatively, grow them in large pots of good quality potting compost.

Varieties

Nowadays the majority of greenhouse cucumbers are all female F1 hybrids and will produce fifteen or more fruits per plant. Many produce traditional long fruits, but there are several shorter varieties.

'Carmen F1' – All female with straight fruits up to 40cm (16in) long. Can withstand some cooler temperatures and has a good resistance to disease.

'Louisa F1' – All female variety that produces long, smooth fruits on disease-resistant plants.

'La Diva' – All female with good cold tolerance that can also be grown outside in a warm, sheltered spot. Produces short, smooth-skinned fruits.

Top: Sowing a single cucumber seed on its side in a pot.
Left: A grafted cucumber plant.

Below left: Cucumbers ready to plant in the polytunnel.
Right: Planting a young cucumber on a slight mound in the soil border.

Sowing and planting

If growing from seed, you need to be able to provide constant warmth through the germination process and while the plants are establishing. I usually sow in my heated greenhouse around late April to produce plants for growing on in the polytunnel from mid-May onwards when temperatures are warmer. In good growing conditions, sowing to planting out should take less than a month.

To germinate, cucumber seeds need a minimum temperature of 20°C, but 25°C is ideal, so a heated propagator is needed. I sow a single seed on its side in a small pot of multipurpose compost and water in. Shoots should start to push through in just a few days and thereafter the plants need to be in good light and warmth.

You can, of course, buy cucumber plants but, again, don't be tempted to buy plants in March or April if you only have a cold greenhouse to grow them in. It's much better to wait until the day and night temperatures in the greenhouse are warmer.

Grafted plants have also become popular over recent years. The benefit is that the plants have more vigour, so you'll get more fruits, and they also have good resistance to some diseases. They are more expensive, but worth it if you've had problems in the past.

Aftercare

Once planted out into the soil border or in large pots, keep the plants warm and out of draughts. They also need to be kept moist at the roots, but not over wet.

Pests and diseases

Red spider mite – The leaves turn brown and often small webs can be seen on the underside. Misting the plants regularly with water will deter them.

White fly – A problem on many greenhouse crops. Yellow sticky traps are effective and you can spray with organic insecticides based on plant oils or soft soaps.

Collar rot – Tends to be worse in spring when the temperatures are cool and the soil around the base of the plants is wet, causing rot to develop at soil level. Initially the plant will wilt a little, giving the appearance that it needs more water. If it is collar rot, the plant will collapse and die. Avoid planting too early in cold conditions and keep the area around the base of the stem dry by planting on a mound.

Root rots – Fungal diseases that attack the roots, usually as a result of wet soil conditions or where cucumbers have been grown for a number of years. Good soil preparation is essential and regular, even watering. Top dress in summer with fresh compost to encourage new roots.

The plants will need support in the form of strings, canes or a frame to grow them up. Tie the main lead stem to the support and as side shoots develop, they also need tying in. Cucumbers can be vigorous and through the summer you may need to trim back excessive growth to keep the plant under control.

Regular feeding is also essential and a high-potash or tomato liquid feed can be given weekly when fruiting starts. If the leaves start to yellow or growth is slow, a couple of high-nitrogen feeds can also be given as a boost. Mulching with fresh compost in mid-summer helps to encourage new roots and supplies extra nutrients.

To maintain humid conditions around the plants, damp paths down with water or mist the plants on a regular basis.

Martin's tips

To help keep the base of the stem dry, sink a plant pot into the soil a few inches away from the plant. When watering, pour directly into the pot rather than round the stem.

Flowers and embryo fruits will start to form while the plant is still small. To help the plant establish, remove any fruits until the plant is at least 60cm (24in) tall.

Whether growing in the border or in pots, plant on a low mound to allow water to drain away from the base of the stem and prevent collar rot.

Harvesting

Fruits will develop quickly and should be picked as soon as they are fully developed and are a glossy green. Once the plant is established in mid-summer, the fruits should start to come thick and fast, so regular picking is essential to encourage more flowers and fruits.

Don't worry if there appear to be marks on the skin of your cucumbers – they're usually caused by the rough underside of the leaf scratching the young fruits.

Powdery mildew – Easily recognised by the white fungal growth on the upper surface of the leaves in late summer. Cut off infected leaves and increase watering and feeding to encourage new growth. Many F1 varieties now have good resistance to it.

Above: Powdery mildew on cucumber leaves.

Above, left: Remove the first few cucumbers to help the plant establish.
Right: Cucumbers starting to develop on the plant.
Left: Small fruited cucumber '**La Diva**'.

Cucumbers in the kitchen

A few years ago Martin and I were lucky enough to be invited to a garden party at Buckingham Palace – it was when he was show director for the Harrogate Flower Shows. Martin was in his element looking round the Queen's gardens but I was blown away by the tea we were given. It was so well organised for the thousands of visitors there on the day. Everything was beautifully served and presented in bite-size portions. As you would expect, there were cucumber sandwiches with the crusts cut off, and they were light, refreshing and very tasty. If ever I make them now, it takes us back to that lovely day! Cucumber sandwiches – by royal appointment.

Cucumber sandwiches

The trick is to dry your cucumber slices a bit first so they don't make the bread soggy, so slice them and leave to dry a little on some kitchen roll.

- Mix a small tub of cream cheese with a good tablespoon of chopped mint and a few chopped chives.
- Spread on thinly sliced brown bread and then layer on some cucumber. To be really fancy I make a triple decker, cut off the crusts and cut them into small squares. Scatter over some more chopped chives.
- For an alternative, try adding some thin slices of strawberry on top of the cucumber and cream cheese with maybe some basil instead of the mint.

Jill's tip

If you're making a dip such as raita or tzatziki using cucumber, then it's important to get rid of as much water as possible, otherwise your dip will quickly get too watery to use. I've found a really great method which is quick, easy and not too messy!

Cut the cucumber in half lengthways then cut in half across. Use a teaspoon to scrape down the length of the cucumber and remove the seeds – easy!

Slice, chop or grate and add to natural yoghurt or sour cream along with some mint, garlic and maybe a bit of parsley or chilli. Serve with sticks of fresh vegetables or crisps.

Cucumber relish

I discovered this recipe years ago when we had a glut of cucumbers coming out of the greenhouse and I was getting desperate! It was so good I quickly made a second batch and have made it ever since. It's one that I always take as a sample to our 'Gardening on the Menu' talk and it seems to go down quite well.

It goes particularly well with a farmhouse loaf and some cheese - Yorkshire Wensleydale and a bit of Appleton's Cheshire are good choices.

A lot of the time is in the preparation of the vegetables in this tasty tangy relish - but it really is worth it. If you have a food processor, then use it rather than grating by hand to save time.

It doesn't last as long as a chutney but the advantage of a relish is that you can eat it just about straight away - try and hang on for a couple of weeks to let the flavours settle in a bit!

Makes about 6 x 225g jars. Takes about 2 hours altogether.

Ingredients and equipment

3 large cucumbers
1 large green pepper, de-seeded and finely diced
2 large onions, grated or finely diced
300g carrots, grated
Good tblsp of salt
Loads of kitchen roll
1 tsp mustard seeds
1 tsp celery seeds
½ tsp ground tumeric
1 litre distilled white vinegar
300g granulated sugar
About 4 tblsps cornflour and 4 tblsps of water
Sterilised jars and lids

Method

- Halve the cucumbers lengthways then use a teaspoon to scrape out the seeds from the middle of the pieces.
- Leaving the skin on, use a coarse grater or food processor to grate the cucumber halves.
- Put into a colander and add in the onions, pepper and grated carrot. Lightly mix together then sprinkle the salt over the mixture.
- Leave for a good hour then rinse under a cold tap, tip out onto kitchen paper and pat dry.
- Scrape everything off the paper and into your preserving pan, then add in the spices, sugar and vinegar.
- Heat gently, stirring until the sugar has dissolved, then bring gently up to a boil, stirring often.
- Turn down the heat to a medium simmer and cook for 30–45 minutes until the liquid has reduced and thickened quite a lot. It will still be runnier than a chutney, though, as the cucumber has such a high water content.
- In a small bowl, add the water to the cornflour and mix together. Stir into the relish and simmer for another 5 minutes until it thickens up.
- Carefully pour into your still warm, sterilised jars. Fill to the top and pop the lids on tightly. Cool and label, then store in a cool, dark place.

This relish should keep for up to a year without losing any flavour. Once you've opened a jar, keep in the fridge and eat within 4–6 weeks.

SARSON'S
VINEGAR

8PTS
7PTS

Quick foot mask

I'm sure many of us have tried a cucumber eye mask for soothing tired and achy eyes but have you considered a cucumber foot mask? Even Martin's been known to try this after a hard day's digging. This remedy really rejuvenates your feet ready for another day in the garden.

In a liquidiser, blitz 1 chopped cucumber along with 2 tblsps of oil and 2 tblsps of lemon juice. Pour into a large shallow bowl and warm slightly in the microwave. Slide your feet in then sit back with a cup of tea or a cucumber cocktail for about ten minutes, then rinse off.

Quick drink – Cucumber fizz

I'm not a gin drinker but I believe there's a cucumber gin that is very refreshing on a hot summer's evening. Or you could try this cocktail that can be alcoholic or not, depending on your taste.

Makes about 6 glasses.

Ingredients

½ cucumber
100ml elderflower cordial
3 or 4 sprigs of mint
1 bottle of prosecco

Method

› Chop the cucumber into pieces and blitz in a liquidiser along with the cordial and the leaves from 2 sprigs of mint. Pour through a sieve, pushing through with the back of a spoon. Stir the puree together and keep in the fridge until ready to use.
› To serve, fill your glasses to about halfway with the puree and top up with prosecco. Stir gently and top with a small sprig of mint.
› For a non-alcoholic version, simply replace the prosecco with lemonade or sparkling mineral water.

Enjoy in the garden on a warm summer's evening with friends!

Leeks in the garden

Leeks are a good vegetable to include in the veg plot because they are fairly easy to grow, are hardy and are in season for at least six months of the year. By growing more than one variety, it is possible to have fresh leeks from the garden from September through until the following May, although in the Fish household we tend to eat them mainly as a winter vegetable between November and March.

When I plant the young seedlings out into the garden in June, I know that come winter we'll be able to enjoy that mild onion flavour and, fortunately, Jill has some lovely leek recipes that have become family favourites.

Soil conditions

Leeks prefer a good, fertile soil that retains moisture in the summer but drains in winter. Heavy clay soils are fine as long as plenty of garden compost or well-rotted manure has been worked into the soil and, likewise, on sandy soil the addition of this bulky organic matter will help to improve the structure. They are fairly greedy, and to produce lovely white leeks, you need to make sure the plants are fed through the growing season with a general fertiliser.

Sowing

If you want early leeks in autumn or for the show bench, sowing can start in February, but for normal kitchen use you can sow later. I sow the seeds in mid to late March which is ideal for producing strong seedlings for planting out in early June.

I used to sow the seed in the traditional way outside in shallow drills and then transplant the

Varieties

Over recent years, more and more leeks have become available to amateur gardeners. These are mainly F1 hybrids that were developed for commercial growing. Some are early or late season and many also have good resistance to rust. There are also some excellent old varieties that are still well worth growing for their hardiness and lovely flavour.

'Musselburgh' – An old variety that has been around since Victorian times. It is very hardy, stands all winter and tastes great.

'Below Zero F1' – A British-bred leek that is very hardy. It produces pure-white shafts, will stand through until May and is resistant to rust.

'Megaton F1' – If you want early leeks, this is the one for you as the shafts are ready to lift from late summer through until mid-autumn.

'Porbella' – A mid-season variety that is best between October and February. It's very hardy and has good resistance to rust.

'Electra' – A good all-rounder that can be used as baby leeks in late summer or left to mature in the garden where it will stand through until March.

Left from top:
Thining leek seedlings in plug trays;
Leek seedlings ready to transplant;
Planting the seedlings with a dibber;
Watering in seedlings.

seedlings, but nowadays I prefer to start them off in plug trays. I find this an easier method and it works well.

The small black, angular seeds are just large enough to handle and I sow a couple of seeds per cell in a plug tray filled with fine multipurpose compost. Ideally, the cells should be around 2.5cm–4.0cm (1.0in–1.5in) in diameter. After filling the tray, I make a shallow depression with a dibber and drop the seeds into it. When watered, compost washes over the seeds. If sowing in mid-March, the seeds should germinate without any problems in a cold greenhouse or cold frame after a couple of weeks.

If both seeds in each cell germinate, once the seedlings are a couple of inches tall, carefully pull out the weakest to allow the other to grow on, making sure you keep the compost in the trays moist at all times.

Planting out and growing on

A couple of months after sowing you should have strong seedlings ready for transplanting out into the garden. To give the seedlings a boost, a week before planting out give them a liquid feed and also sprinkle some general fertiliser on the plot of land where you are going to plant.

When it comes to planting out, I still use the traditional method of planting in deep holes to blanch the base of the stem so that we get long white shafts in winter.

Using a dibber, make holes in the prepared soil approximately 10cm–15cm (4in–6in) deep, 20cm (8in) apart, and pop a leek seedling into the hole so that half of it is below soil level. Water each seedling by pouring water into the hole to settle the roots. If the weather is dry, you might need to water again in a week or so to make sure the soil in the base of the hole stays moist.

Through the summer, keep the plants weed free at all times. If using a hoe, take care not to damage the leek stem. Although planting in holes blanches the base of the leek, earthing them up slightly in late summer will give a longer white shaft. I usually give a final feed of general fertiliser in August and then pull a warren hoe between the rows of leeks to create a ridge against the shafts. If you haven't got a warren hoe (this is a great tool for making deep drills or earthing up), a Dutch or draw hoe can be used.

In early autumn when the leeks are almost fully grown, pick through them and remove any dead leaves. This makes them look better and, more importantly, helps to prevent fungal diseases in winter.

Above: Removing dead foliage from around the base of leeks.

Harvesting

Harvesting can start as soon as the leeks are large enough to eat. I use a garden fork to gently lever out the roots. To trim the leeks, use a knife to slice off the roots and trim back the green leaves, but don't cut the green back completely, as the leaves can also be eaten.

Leeks are hardy and can withstand frost, so I tend to lift them as we need them through the winter months. If heavy frost is forecast and the ground is likely to freeze solid, I'll lift some, trim the roots and tops and pop them in the fridge.

Pests and diseases

Leek rust – This is probably the most common disease of leeks, but it can also attack onions, garlic and chives. It is easily recognisable by the orange pustules that develop on the leaves from mid-summer onward. There are no fungicides available to control it. Good garden hygiene and not composting diseased material will help. Do not over-feed plants with nitrogen as this encourages soft, lush leaves that are more prone to attack. Instead

Above: Trimming leeks before taking into the kitchen.

Martin's tips

If I have plenty of seedlings, I often plant a row closely together, say 5.0cm–7.5cm (2in–3in) apart, to harvest in late summer as baby leeks, which always gets me brownie points with Jill in the kitchen!

Occasionally a few leeks will produce a flower stalk. When this appears, remove it straight away and eat the leek as soon as possible because if left in the ground, it will develop a hard core

use a balanced general feed containing potash. Some varieties have good resistance to the disease.

Leek moth – This is becoming an increasing problem for leek growers and is gradually moving north from the south-west up through the midlands. So far, I don't think it's arrived in North Yorkshire, but I suspect it's only a matter of time. The small moth lays eggs on young leeks and the caterpillars cause a great deal of damage by eating the foliage and the centre of the plant. No insecticides are available to gardeners and the only sure way to protect leeks in areas where it is a problem is to grow them under fleece or fine mesh.

Leeks can also be affected by other diseases that attack onions, such as white rot and downy mildew. See '**Onions**' for more details.

Top: Orange pustules on leek leaves - sure sign of rust.
Above, left: Leek moth damage.
Right: Leeks can be harvested throughout the winter months.

Leeks in the kitchen

Leeks keep me going over the winter months with their sweet, mild, oniony flavour. I love them and they're so versatile – I use them in casseroles, pies, stocks and bakes and I always make batches of soup for the freezer. They steam well, usually taking about eight minutes, or you can pan fry or simmer sliced leeks in water or some stock.

Generally, I don't freeze them uncooked as they tend to go a bit mushy, but if I've got some spare or my recipe only uses the white of the leek, I slice the leftovers and sauté them in a little butter for four or five minutes. After cooling they can be frozen and then used for casseroles or soup.

I've found that home-grown leeks need very little cleaning – it must be the way Martin grows them – but if there is a bit of soil inside the layers, then just slice them and wash in a sieve. If you're chopping them or using in soup, then cut them in half lengthways and wash the outer layers before use. The white part of the leek is the best for eating on its own but the first bit of the green can be used for slower cooking in casseroles and soups.

Easy cook - Buttery leeks

Our favourite way of eating them is really simple. I slice them quite thinly and pop a knob of butter in a pan to melt. Stir the leeks in so that they all get a coating, grind over some salt and pepper then put the lid on the pan and pop on a low heat to cook for about 15 minutes, stirring occasionally. They cook in their own buttery juices and I serve them alongside some creamy mashed potatoes with some slices of roast chicken and gravy. Mmm!

Opposite page, left top: Lovely buttery leeks.
Bottom: Leek, potato and ham gratin.

Above from top: Leek and seafood pancakes: use a selection of fish and try to include some smoked fish; a pancake with fish and leek filling before popping into the oven to finish off cooking.

Seafood and leek pancakes – not just for Pancake Day!

Add a little extra flavour to your pancakes by adding some snipped chives (this works well with all sorts of herbs and spices, depending on what you're serving your pancakes with).

Makes 4 pancakes - 2 each

Takes about 50 minutes

Ingredients

For the chive pancakes:

Makes 8 pancakes - 4 for this recipe and 4 for a sweet treat afterwards!
100g plain flour
Pinch of salt
1 medium egg
275ml milk
Tblsp chopped chives

For the filling:

320g pack of mixed fish, cut into bite-sized pieces
About 10 large cooked prawns
450ml milk
1 bay leaf
Salt and pepper
1 leek, sliced
25g butter
25g plain flour
Tblsp of chopped chives
50g Gruyère cheese, grated

Method

To make the pancakes:

› Make the batter in the usual way - mix the salt with the flour in a large bowl, make a well in the middle and drop the egg into it. Gradually stir the egg in and add the milk a little at a time until all the flour is worked in. Beat well, put half the batter on one side to make pancakes for pudding then stir the chives into the remaining batter.
› Heat a little oil in a frying pan and pour in some batter to coat the base of the pan. When golden brown, flip over to cook the other side. Turn out onto greaseproof paper and repeat to make four pancakes.

To make the filling:

› Pour the milk into a pan and add the mixed fish, bay leaf and a grinding of salt and pepper. Bring to a gentle simmer and poach for 5 minutes. Turn off the heat and leave in the milk for about 20 minutes. Drain, removing the bay leaf and saving the milk.
› Heat the butter in a frying pan and cook the leeks for about 5 minutes until softened.
› Stir in the flour and cook for a couple of minutes. Remove from the heat and gradually add the milk used for poaching, stirring all the time. Return to the heat and bring to a simmer, stirring constantly.
› Simmer until the sauce has thickened, then add the fish, prawns and the chives. Stir gently to coat.

To assemble the dish:

› Lay a pancake flat and add a good spoonful of the fish mixture. Spread out then carefully fold in half, then in quarters.
› Transfer to a circular ovenproof dish and repeat with the other three pancakes. Spread any remaining sauce over the top and sprinkle over the cheese.
› Pop in the oven, 180°C (fan 160°C) gas 4, for about 20 minutes until the cheese is golden brown.

Cheesy leek and bacon puff

Cheese and leeks go really well together and this puff pastry treat is a perfect combination of flavours. It's a really good picnic or buffet dish as when served at room temperature, the filling stays intact. You could make it into individual parcels and try different additions to the fillings – some mushrooms or chunks of cooked potato, maybe? We enjoy it served hot with a serving of baked beans on the side!

Ingredients

2 tblsp oil
8 rashers bacon
25g butter
4 medium leeks, thinly sliced
2 tsps thyme leaves
140g Gruyère cheese, cut into small cubes
1 large egg, beaten with a little water
500g pack puff pastry

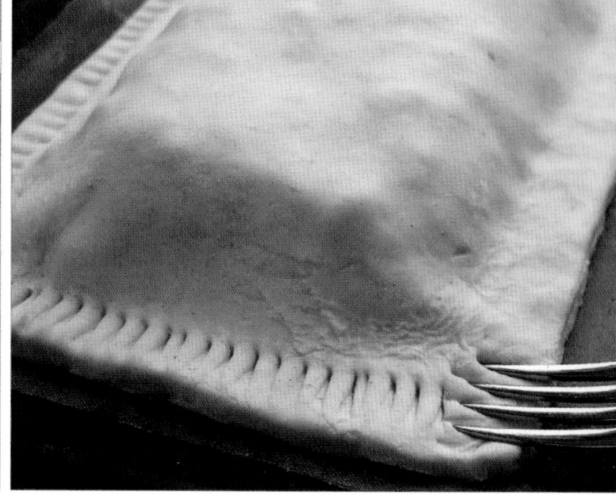

Above: Cheesy leek and bacon puff - excellent for picnics or a light supper.

Method

- Heat 1tblsp of the oil in a frying pan. Trim the rind off the bacon and cut into small pieces. Fry until beginning to crisp. Remove from the pan and pat off any excess oil with kitchen paper.
- Heat the remaining oil and the butter in the pan and add the leeks, thyme and seasoning. Cook until softened.
- Put the leeks, bacon and cheese in a bowl and mix lightly. Leave to cool.
- Cut off one third of the pastry and roll into a 15cm x 30cm rectangle. Place on a lightly greased baking tray.
- Pile the cheesy leek and bacon filling onto the rolled pastry, leaving a 2cm border all around.
- Roll the remaining pastry into a larger rectangle - so that it will cover the base.
- Brush the edges of the base with the egg then top with the larger rectangle of pastry. Smooth down gently to get rid of air pockets. Cut away any excess pastry to make a tidy edge then brush all over with the egg wash.
- Seal the edges really well with a fork, and cover and chill for at least 30 minutes.
- When ready to cook, brush with more egg wash and season with a little salt and pepper.
- Pop into a preheated oven, 200°C (fan 180°C), gas 6, for 10 minutes then reduce the heat to 180°C (fan 160°C), gas 4, and cook for another 25–30 minutes until puffed up and golden brown.

Serve straight away or enjoy at room temperature later in the day.

Quick cook – Crispy leeks

If you've made some leek and potato soup, then top it with some crispy leeks as a garnish. Slice leeks into thin strips - as long as you fancy - then toss in some oil. Sprinkle over some flour seasoned with a bit of paprika, salt and pepper and maybe some garlic powder, then spread out on a baking sheet. Pop in a hot oven, 220°C (fan 200°C), gas 7, for about 10–12 minutes until they're golden brown and crispy. Watch them, though, as if they go past being caramelised, they will taste quite bitter.

Jill's tip

If Martin's had a good germination, then we plant a patch of leeks more densely so that we can use the baby leeks in the kitchen. They have such a delicate taste and as it's such a limited season, they're a real treat.

Easy cook – Leek, ham and potato gratin

As well as being really easy, you can make this dish ahead and freeze or keep overnight before cooking. See picture on p112.

Serves 2

Takes about an hour and a quarter

- Pour 140ml mix of stock (ham, chicken or veg) and milk and 75ml of double cream into a pan and add in a good handful of chopped thyme and rosemary and a crushed clove of garlic. Bring this to a boil then turn off and leave to infuse the flavours.
- Slice a good-sized leek and mix together with enough peeled and sliced potato to feed two. Add in some chopped cooked ham and pile into a greased, shallow baking dish.
- Pour over the sauce, trying to cover as much as possible, then scatter over some grated cheddar cheese.
- Cover loosely with tinfoil and pop in the oven, 180°C (fan 160°C), gas 4, for about an hour - take the tinfoil off for the last 15 minutes or so to brown the top.

You could use any meat you have in this dish, it works really well with some sliced chorizo or leave out completely.

Easy cook – baby leeks

All you need to do is wash and trim the baby leeks then melt a little butter in a frying pan and roll them around to coat, then add in some stock to cover and some thyme leaves, then leave to poach gently for about 20 minutes.

Serve simply with roast chicken and mashed potato - yum!

Or you could roast them - blanch first for a couple of minutes in boiling water then drain really well. Toss in olive oil and a bit of garlic then season and pop in a roasting tray in a single layer. Roast for about 10 minutes at 200°C (fan 180°C), gas 6, but keep an eye on them as they catch on the edges really quickly!

Onions, shallots and garlic in the garden

I grow onions purely for the kitchen, not the show bench. However, some of my first experiences of growing onions were with my Uncle on his allotment and he always grew 'Kelsae' onions for showing. The seed was always sown on Boxing Day – the things people do to get out of washing up! Following in Uncle Arthur's footsteps, as a young man I did a little veg exhibiting at village shows and although I say it myself, I always did all right with onions!

We eat a lot of onions and I always grow a few different types in the garden each year to get a variety of flavours. Some are mild and others are strong! I grow from seed and sets, and as well as bulb onions I also grow shallots, garlic and a few spring onions.

Soil conditions

All members of the onion family (Allium), including shallots and garlic, grow best in a sunny position, on well-drained soil that has been well prepared in advance. My onion plot is planted where brassicas were grown the previous season. The onions can take advantage of the fact that the brassica roots have broken up the soil and they will also benefit from the lime that would have been applied to raise the pH (alkalinity) for the brassicas. I also dig in plenty of organic matter in late winter and allow the soil to naturally break down by spring. Just before planting, I give the soil a dressing of general fertiliser to give them a good start.

From top:
Sowing onion seeds in the greenhouse; onion sets being started in trays; and planting onion sets into the ground in spring.

Varieties

Catalogues have a good selection of sets or seed to choose from and will usually recommend varieties that are good keepers.

From sets

'Sturon' – Very reliable, producing good-sized onions with a fine flavour. Doesn't tend to bolt and the bulbs store well.

'Centurion' – A heavy cropper with slightly flattened bulbs and good flavour. Stores very well over winter.

'Stuttgarter' – An old variety, but still widely grown because it grows and stores well.

'Red Baron' – A popular red onion with a mild flavour that will store well when fully ripe. Can bolt if planted when the soil is cold. This variety is also available from seed.

'Electric' – A red onion for autumn planting with pink flesh that can be harvested in June.

'Radar' – A white-fleshed, autumn-planted onion with a mild flavour ready to pull in July.

Onions

Sowing and planting

Onions can be grown from seed or from sets, which are small, immature bulbs that when planted, complete their growth cycle. Sets can be planted in spring to harvest in early autumn and these are known as main-crop onions. You can also plant overwintering onion sets in September that are ready to harvest the following June and July for an early crop.

For bulb onions, the seeds can be sown between January and March in gentle heat. I normally sow my seeds in late January or early February in a small seed tray filled with a mix of half John Innes and half multipurpose compost. I find this works well for onions. They are germinated at a temperature of around 13°C-15°C - if it's a lot warmer, the seeds don't always germinate properly. The seedlings are ideally pricked out into cell trays at what is known as the crook stage, which is when the top of the seed leaf is still looped over. The seedlings are grown on in the greenhouse or polytunnel in cool conditions until they are ready to plant out into

Martin's tips

- When planting onion sets, firm them into the soil, otherwise birds may pull them out.
- If you want small onions for cooking, plant three sets close together in a cell tray and plant out as a clump after they have grown a few inches. Instead of one large onion, you get three small ones in a clump.

Varieties/cont...

From seed

'Robinson's Mammoth' – A large onion that is often used on the show bench, but also great for the garden. Produces large, mild-flavoured bulbs.

'Santero F1' – A good, medium-sized onion with good flavour. Also has excellent resistance to downy mildew.

'Bedfordshire Champion' – An old tried-and-tested variety producing large onions that are great for the kitchen and if kept cold, will store through winter.

'Kelsae' – One of the most popular for showing. Produces large, pale onions with a mild flavour. Not a long keeper.

'Arthur F1' – This hybrid produces uniform bulbs with good skin colour and great flavour. The bulbs also store well through winter.

Spring onion **'White Lisbon'** – An old variety, but very reliable and will produce tasty spring onions for much of the year if sown in succession.

the garden, which is usually around mid-to-late April when the soil is starting to warm up.

Spring or salad onions tend to be sown directly into the ground in shallow drills through the spring and early summer. Many can also be sown outside in September to overwinter. These are pulled when small and tender for use in salads or cooking and often have a mild flavour.

Sets are a much simpler way to grow onions and can be planted directly into the prepared ground from early April onwards. I use a small trowel to plant the sets so that the tip is just visible. I space them approximately 15cm (6in) apart with the rows around 30cm (12in) apart.

Alternatively, when soil conditions are not suitable to plant out, the sets can be started off in cell trays of compost under cover. Allow them to make a good root system and top growth before transplanting them into the garden.

Aftercare

If the weather is dry after planting, water the roots to help them establish. Keep the bed weed free to prevent the young plants being smothered by weeds and to improve air circulation. If using a hoe, take care not to damage the stems.

In the summer when the bulbs are swelling, I like to give a couple of liquid feeds with a balanced fertiliser to keep the plants growing without a check in growth.

Occasionally onions will bolt (produce a flowering stem). This can be caused by a change in weather and there's nothing you can do to prevent it. As soon as the flower appears, pinch it off and eat those onions first as they

Spring onion **'Apache'** – A fast-growing red spring onion that is great in salads and stir fries.

Martin's tip

Some onion sets are specially heat treated before they are packaged to prevent them from bolting during the summer.

Pests and diseases

Onions can be attacked by various problems and below are some of the more common ones that attack members of the onion family. Good growing conditions, crop rotation and garden hygiene will always help to reduce risk.

Downy mildew (*see image opposite*) – A fungal disease that starts at the tips and works its way down the foliage. It is worse in wet, humid weather. No treatments are available. If it's a problem, try growing 'Santero' which has some resistance. It's worth noting that the spores can overwinter on autumn-planted onions and infect spring-planted onions.

Top: Pinch off onion flower heads as soon as they form.
Bottom: Onion downy mildew.

Top: Bent over onion tops to help ripening.
Bottom: Easing out the roots with a fork to stop growth.

don't store as well once they have bolted.

In late summer when the tops are starting to die back, bend the leaves over to expose the bulbs to maximum light to help with the natural ripening process.

Harvesting and storing

Onions can be harvested through the summer if needed, but if you intend to store them over winter, they need to fully ripen. Once they have stopped growing and the tops are dying back, use a fork to loosen the roots. This stops them taking in water and helps with ripening. If the weather is dry, leave the onions to ripen outside, but if damp, lift them and dry in an airy place until the outer skins are dry and brittle.

When ripe, onions will store for several months although some varieties store better than others. The large exhibition onions don't store as long and should be eaten first.

Onions can be stored in trays or on traditional strings and hung in a dry, frost-proof shed or garage over winter. Check them regularly and remove any that are starting to rot.

White rot – Probably the most serious onion disease you can get. The leaves turn yellow and wilt and white fungal mould develops on the base of the bulb. The spores stay in the soil for up to ten years and there is no control. Filling raised beds with fresh soil is one way to be able to grow onions, but the spores transfer very easily on tools.

Onion neck rot – Mainly a problem on onions being stored but can also affect growing bulbs. Fungal growths develop and the neck of the bulb softens and rots. To try to avoid, do not overfeed and encourage soft growth after mid-summer, and allow the bulbs to fully ripen in dry conditions. Buy sets and seeds from a reputable supplier as spores can be carried on them.

Onion thrips – A fine mottling appears on the leaves caused by the tiny flies sucking sap. Usually worse in hot, dry weather. Organic insecticides based on plant oils will help to control if started early in the season, but if the infestation is light, the onions will be fine. Thrips can also be a problem on leeks.

As a rule, onions tend to store much better if the summer has been warm, especially at the end of the growing season.

Shallots

These are ideal for cooking and pickling. They are normally grown from sets, although seed is available for some varieties. Shallots are hardy and require a long growing season. Some books recommend planting on the shortest day and harvesting on the longest. Although sets can be planted directly into the garden, I start them into growth in the polytunnel in cell trays in late February. Once they have made a good root system and leaves, I plant them out into the garden approximately 15cm-20cm (6in-8in) apart in late March and they grow away very quickly.

The clumps of shallots are lifted from the plot in late summer once the tops have died down and, as long as they are ripe, they will store through the winter until needed. You can also save some of the best bulbs to re-plant the following season.

Right: Planting out shallots from cell trays in spring.

Opposite page
Top: Garlic plants ready to plant out.
Bottom: The onion bed in late summer.

Onion fly – Tiny maggots eat the roots and the plant collapses. There are no treatments available. Seed-grown plants are more likely to be attacked than onion sets. Cover plants with horticultural fleece to keep the adult flies off.

Varieties - shallots

'Golden Gourmet' – A good, reliable variety that produces clumps of golden bulbs.

'Zebrune' – An old variety that has long, narrow bulbs with a pink tinge.

'Bistro' – A heavy cropping variety with golden, round bulbs that have a mild, sweet flavour.

Garlic

It's often thought that garlic only grows in hot countries, but it is surprisingly tough and needs a cold period to grow well. Having said that, it likes a sunny spot with well-drained soil for the summer months.

The bulbs break down to around ten to twelve individual cloves and these can be planted into the garden in October or November around 5cm (2in) deep where they will produce a root system and short growth. Come spring when the temperature warms up, they will grow away and make tall foliage.

Alternatively, the cloves can be potted into small pots or cell trays and started into growth in a cold frame, cold greenhouse or polytunnel in autumn or winter to produce plants for planting out in March or April.

Garlic is fairly simple to grow and in good soil and with a long growing season will produce good-sized bulbs. Garlic doesn't seem to be troubled by too many problems, although rust can be a problem and it often bolts. However, this doesn't seem to affect it too much and they still produce a bulb underground.

Harvest the garlic when the tops turn yellow and store in a cool, dry shed over winter.

Varieties

Although garlic bought in a supermarket will grow, it doesn't always produce good bulbs. I think it's much better to buy named varieties that are suitable for growing in our climate and are certified virus free.

Hardneck varieties are said to be the best choice for northern gardens because they are hardier than softneck types, but I've grown both types by starting them off in pots in the polytunnel.

'Red Duke' – A hardneck type with white skin and purple cloves.

'Caulk Wight' – A purple-skinned hardneck type that is very hardy.

'Solent Wight' – Large white bulbs of softneck garlic that store very well.

Left, Planting garlic cloves in pots to start them into growth.

Opposite page: Freshly harvested garlic.

Onions, shallots and garlic in the kitchen

Cheese and onion - perfect together in so many ways. My favourite combination has to be in a cheese and onion pasty, just warm, straight from the oven. Here in Yorkshire we have Thomas the Bakers who make the most fantastic pasties and I have to confess this is one of my guilty pleasures - don't tell Martin!

Onions have so many uses in the kitchen that I can't possibly do them justice here. They are often just used as a base to a recipe and have to take second place to other ingredients, perhaps in a soup, casserole or sauce, but here I'm sharing some onion recipes where onions can really take centre stage.

Jill's tip

So many recipes call for a cooked onion and it often states 'do not allow to colour'. Ideally, you're looking for a translucent effect which will give the most flavour to your dish and this is the base for most pasta sauces, soups and casseroles. The best way is long and slow. Melt a knob of butter with a glug of oil in a shallow pan over a low heat until the butter just starts to sizzle. Add in your finely chopped onion and stir to coat. Leave to cook for about ten minutes on a fairly low heat.

Opposite page: Enjoy red onion marmalade with some creamy brie

Onions

Roasted feta stuffed onions

You don't tend to see stuffed onions on the menu very often nowadays, which is a shame. They have a lovely creamy texture with a mild taste that make them great for eating on their own, stuffed with a variety of fillings. This is a vegetarian version but you could just as easily fill them with some bolognaise sauce or chilli.

Serves 2, 2 onions each

Takes about an hour

Ingredients

4 medium onions, a mixture of red and white looks good
Good glug of oil
125g feta cheese, crumbled
½ red chilli, de-seeded and diced
3 or 4 pieces sun-dried tomato, chopped small
35g breadcrumbs
35g pine nuts
1 small egg, beaten
3 or 4 sprigs thyme leaves

Method

› Don't peel the onions, just trim the top and break off any long dirty roots and loose layers of dried skin. Bring a large pan of water to the boil and pop the onions in so that they are fully submerged. Simmer gently for about 10-15 minutes until they feel tender but firm enough to handle.
› Drain, then cover in cold water for a few minutes then drain again.
› When the onions are cool enough to handle, slice off the top couple of centimetres and peel away the outside layers of skin. Use a knife to trim the roots, leaving enough root to hold the onion together.
› Carefully scoop out several layers from the middle of the onion with a knife or a teaspoon and chop finely.
› Mix the chopped onion in a bowl along with the pine nuts, tomato, chilli, parsley and 100g of the feta cheese. Add the breadcrumbs and the beaten egg along with a good grinding of salt and pepper and mix together well.
› Place the onions in a smallish ovenproof dish so that they fit snugly. Spoon the filling into each onion, packing it in well. Pile it up fairly high to use all the mixture. Scatter over the remaining feta. Drizzle with the oil.

› Cover loosely with foil and pop in the oven, 200°C (fan 180°C), gas 6, for 25 minutes. Remove the foil and leave in for a further 10 minutes until the feta is browning on top.

Boiling the onions before stuffing is the quickest method but you could roast them for this recipe too. Peel and halve the onions then remove several layers from the inside of each one. Brush them with some olive oil and put a little water in the base of the dish. Tightly cover with foil and bake in a medium oven, 180°C (fan 140°C), gas 4, for about 50 minutes. Chop the inside layers and fry to use in the feta stuffing.

Jill's tip

I put a thickly sliced onion under most of my roasts. The meat sits on top of the slices which cook down, adding real flavour to the meat juices. Crush into the gravy to release all the flavours. If you want a smooth-textured gravy, simply pass through a sieve before serving.

Jill's tips

The Big Question!

So many people ask how to chop onions without tears in their eyes! There are all sorts of methods and gadgets but I don't think anything works completely. Personally, I favour the fast and furious method! You produce tears because your eyes are reacting protectively to the irritant gas that's released on chopping, so don't linger on the chopping!

I tend to chop my onion in half through the roots then use a sharp knife to cut the root away, at arm's length, and throw it away. Then move to a different bit of the kitchen! Peel the onions then slice as required. For fine chopping, I cut each half in thin slices across the onion then chop lengthways without disturbing the slices.

Red onion marmalade

We seemed to grow a load of red onions this year so I decided to make a batch of red onion marmalade. Fortunately, we went to the Nidderdale Agricultural Show a few days before and I found myself watching a demonstration of a mandolin slicer and decided it was time to invest. I'm so glad I did! Once I'd got the hang of it, it saved me loads of time slicing the onions and seemed to keep the tears at bay for a while as well!

I'm never quite sure why this is called a marmalade but it's very tasty and is great with burgers, sausages or a chunk of mature cheddar. It's also handy to add to gravy or a casserole for an added depth of flavour.

Makes about 6 large jars

Takes about an hour plus slicing time!

Ingredients

4 tblsps oil
2kg red onions (white can be used too)
300g light-brown muscovado sugar
300ml red wine vinegar
250ml red wine
3 tblsps balsamic vinegar
3 garlic cloves, crushed
2 tsps wholegrain mustard
Good pinch paprika
Half chilli, chopped finely
2 bay leaves
Salt and pepper
Sterilised jars and lids

Method

- First job is to slice the onions as thinly as possible - I'd recommend a mandolin!
- Heat the oil in your jam pan and pile in the onions - there will appear to be a huge amount but they soon cook down. Fry gently over a medium heat for about 10 minutes.
- Add 100g of the sugar and cook for another 10–15 minutes until the onions are really soft. Stir every now and again to avoid them sticking. The onions will release lots of lovely juices.
- Add all the other ingredients and simmer for 35–40 minutes until most of the liquid has evaporated. Stir regularly.
- Pot into your hot jars and seal immediately.
- Keep in a cool, dark place. Once opened, keep in the fridge.

Top: Sticky onion hot dogs.
Centre: Blanching shallots in hot water for a minute makes peeling easier.
Bottom: Frying shallots before adding to a stew.

Quick cook – Sticky onion hot dogs

This is a great TV supper or one to have outside with a bonfire.

Cut a couple of peeled onions into fairly thin wedges and pop in a small roasting tray with a good tablespoon of balsamic vinegar and a tablespoon of soft brown sugar. Mix together but don't break up the wedges. Put four thick, meaty sausages on top then roast in the oven, 220°C (fan 200°C), gas 7, for about 25-30 minutes. Give everything a stir round a couple of times during cooking so the onions don't stick. I like to cut the sausages in half lengthways at this point so the oniony flavours really add to the sausages. Add a good dash or two of Yorkshire's Henderson's Relish or Worcestershire sauce and leave for another 5-10 minutes or so until the sausages are cooked through. If the onions do start to catch, add in a dash or two of stock or hot water.

Serve in hot-dog rolls with everything piled onto the bread. Don't forget to scrape out the pan juices onto the top of the sausages.

Shallots

The taste of shallots is much sweeter and milder than onions and they can be added raw to salads or dressings. They can be pan fried or roasted in a little butter or olive oil then simmered in stock or flavours such as balsamic vinegar, honey, red wine or orange juice.

They work really well in a stew or casserole. Add at the beginning so that they almost melt away or in the last half an hour after browning in a pan so that they still have some bite.

Quick cooks

- Gently fry some sliced shallots in a little butter then toss into some cooked green beans.
- Use some buttery shallots to top some creamy mashed potato.

Jill's tip

For easy peeling, just trim the top and a little around the root and put in a heatproof bowl. Pour over boiling water and leave for one minute. Drain then cover in cold water. You'll find the skins peel away really easily, saving you loads of fiddly time.

Spring onions

Spring onions are great to add a bit of a kick to salads and salsas, but have a go at grilling them or try them on the barbecue for a change. They are creamy and mild and taste lovely with some flavoured mayonnaise or just a squeeze of lemon juice.

Jill's tip

Use spring onions with your noodles – mix together some chopped spring onion and some diced green chilli then stir in a squeeze of lime juice and some zest. Leave to flavour up for at least half an hour then stir through hot noodles.

Quick cook – Griddled spring onions with spring onion mayonnaise

Brush a trimmed bunch of spring onions with oil then pop on a medium-heat griddle or grill. Cook, turning once, for about 10–15 minutes until creamily tender, covering for the last half of cooking time, if you can.

Make a flavoured mayonnaise to serve with them by adding two finely chopped spring onions and a tablespoon of chopped coriander to 100g of mayonnaise.

Above: A handy 'gadget' for mincing garlic cloves.

Jill's tips

- If you need to crush individual cloves, there are all sorts of gadgets available and I found a good one at a food show I went to last year. You just rub the clove over the little grooves and it minces it immediately. Washing up is a doddle and there's no waste.
- For easy removal of the skin, simply squash the clove lightly with the back of a knife.

Garlic

Home-grown garlic has such a fantastic flavour and it keeps for ages in store as long as there is proper air circulation. I use garlic in loads of dishes but my favourite has to be garlic bread.

Quick cook – Garlic bread

I like to roast my garlic first as it brings out the flavour and sweetness of the garlic. Take off the outer papery skin and cut the top off the bulb to just expose the cloves. Wrap loosely with tinfoil and roast slowly, 160°C (fan 140°C), gas3, for about an hour until the garlic feels soft. Allow to cool and squeeze the cloves to release the lovely paste. Mix with some butter then spread over warm French bread or ciabatta.

Quick cook – Garlic and lemon chicken

Use garlic to make a stuffing for chicken for an easy supper dish.

For each chicken breast, put a good knob of butter into a bowl with the zest of half a lemon, a good handful of chopped parsley and a crushed garlic clove. Stir together.

Make three cuts into your chicken breast then stuff them with the flavoured butter. Season, then put into a small roasting dish and squeeze over some lemon juice. Roast in the oven, 190°C (fan 170°C), gas 5, for about 25 minutes until the chicken is cooked through.

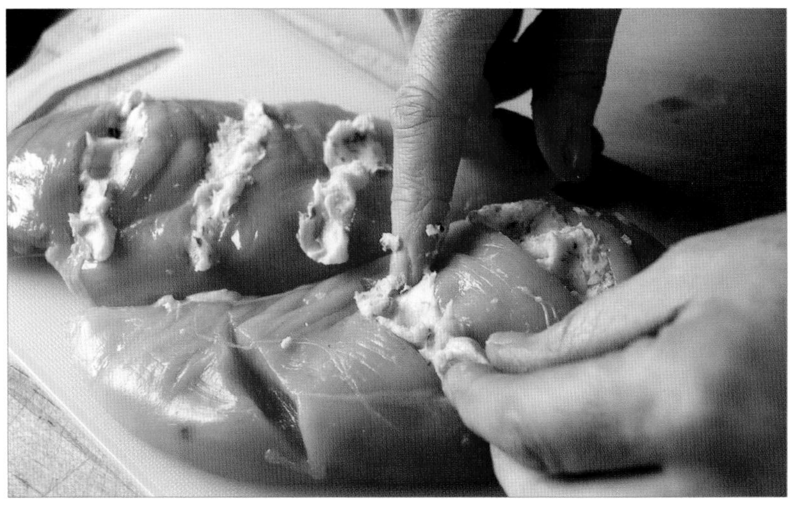

Parsnips and carrots in the garden

Roast dinners in the winter certainly wouldn't be the same without roast parsnips! We love that sweet taste and Jill cooks them in a variety of ways to bring out the flavour. Parsnips are grown in the root bed and are fairly easy to grow. They are totally hardy and can stay in the ground all winter long and be lifted as you need them for the kitchen. Many people don't start lifting the roots until after we've had a few frosts which is supposed to sweeten them slightly, but I'm not sure it makes that much difference! I think the sweetness comes from growing the root fast and in good soil conditions. I grow a couple of rows which keeps us well supplied, and on our well-drained sandy-loam, they grow very well.

Although we eat them mainly through the winter months, they are so tasty I could eat them at any time of the year, in fact we often pull a few in early autumn!

Soil conditions

To grow well, parsnips and carrots prefer a deep, light, sandy soil to allow the roots to grow straight down. Heavy, clay soils will grow root crops, but they need to have been improved the previous season by adding in plenty of garden compost or well-rotted manure to open up the soil structure. Never add fresh compost or manure to the soil before sowing parsnips or carrots as it will cause the roots to fork.

A general fertiliser can be applied to the ground before sowing, but avoid fertilisers high in nitrogen as this encourages lots of leaf growth and poor roots.

Parsnips

Sowing and planting

People sow their parsnips in a variety of ways. Some start the seeds off on damp kitchen paper to germinate and others start their parsnips off in old toilet rolls in a greenhouse and then plant out when the seedlings are a few inches tall. I always say, gardening isn't an exact science and if it works for you, stick with it!

I sow my parsnips directly into the garden and it works very well for me. If sowing this way, the secret is not to sow too early. Old gardening books often refer to sowing in February to give the plants a long growing season, but very often the seed would sit there in cold, wet soil and rot off. It's much better to wait until the soil is naturally warming up and not too wet. This way the seeds will germinate much faster and grow away without a check in growth, and be much sweeter!

Early to mid-April is when I sow. After the soil has been prepared and raked to form a seed bed, I draw out a drill approximately 1.5cm (3/4in) deep. If the soil is starting to dry out, I water along the base of the drill before sowing. A few seeds are sown in groups on the wet soil approximately 7.5cm-10cm (3in-4in) apart along the row. The seeds are then covered over by carefully raking fine soil over them and I finish off by gently tamping down the soil over the seeds with the back of the rake.

Varieties

There are several very good F1 hybrids to choose from and if canker is a problem in your garden, look out for those with some resistance.

'Gladiator F1' – Very popular due to its smooth skin, sweet roots and resistance to canker.

'White Gem' – An old variety that produces medium-sized cream roots and good flavour.

'Countess F1' – Regarded as one of the sweetest parsnips, it has smooth roots and good resistance to canker.

'Palace F1' – A very good cropping parsnip that produces long, pale roots with a sweet flavour. It also has good resistance to canker and is the one I've grown for the past couple of years with great success.

Martin's tip

Don't be tempted to sow the remains of last year's seed packet! Parsnip seed doesn't keep once opened, so always start with a fresh packet each year.

Top: Sow parsnip seeds in shallow drills and then lightly rake over fine soil before tamping down.
Bottom: Once the seedlings reach a height of a couple of inches, carefully thin them out.

Growing and aftercare

In the correct conditions, seedlings should start to pop through the soil in a couple of weeks, but they can sometimes take a little longer, so be patient! If weed seedlings start to grow, carefully pull them out by hand to prevent them smothering the young parsnips. When they are a couple of inches tall, thin the groups of parsnip seedlings. Hopefully, most will have germinated and where you have a cluster of seedlings, you need to remove all but the strongest to grow on.

Through the summer, keep the row weeded and water only in dry conditions while the seedlings are establishing.

If the soil was prepared and fertilised before sowing, there's no need to give any more feed as they don't require high nutrient levels.

Harvesting and storing

You can start pulling roots as soon as they are large enough to eat, which is usually early autumn. Being hardy, they can stay in the soil over winter and be lifted as you need them. Small roots can be pulled out by hand, but if they have grown long, it's a good idea to use a fork to loosen the soil and avoid the roots snapping off.

If carrot root fly is a problem in your plot, bear in mind that roots left in the soil over winter are more prone to damage. Roots can be lifted in early winter and stored in buckets of damp sand for winter use.

Pests and diseases

Parsnip canker – This is a fungal disease that develops cankers (rough areas) on the shoulders and roots that are usually a rusty colour or black. Damage caused by carrot root fly is often how the spores enter the roots and the two problems go hand in hand. There are no treatments, but late sowings and smaller roots are often less susceptible to damage. The roots are still fine to eat once the canker is peeled off.
If canker is a problem, grow varieties with resistance.

Violet root rot – This fungal disease tends only to be a problem in very wet, acid soil conditions. The foliage turns yellow and when the roots are lifted, they are covered in purple strands. There are no treatments and if you are unlucky enough to suffer this problem, burn the roots and improve the soil.

Carrot root fly – This is a big problem on carrots, but it also attacks parsnips. The adult fly lays eggs in the soil at the base of the plants and the small grubs (larvae) eat into the roots, causing brown tunnels, ruining the crop. There are no soil

Martin's tip

If very frosty weather is forecast, it's a good idea to cover over the row with straw or a mulch of leaves to prevent the ground from freezing, allowing you to dig the roots.

Top: Healthy roots of Parsnip 'Palace F1'
Bottom: Parsnip canker and carrot root fly damage.

Top: Sowing carrot seeds thinly along a shallow drill.
Centre: Seedlings being thinned.
Bottom: Holding back the foliage to get water down into the roots.

Carrots

There's nothing nicer than a crunchy carrot pulled fresh from the garden, especially when the first baby carrots of the season are ready.

Being a root crop, the seeds are always best sown directly into their cropping position as the seedlings do not like being transplanted. By making several sowings through the season, it's possible to have fresh carrots from late spring through until winter and if you have a greenhouse or polytunnel, you can get them even earlier.

The main problem for many gardeners, including me, is the dreaded carrot root fly. This pest can ruin a crop and over the years I've tried all sorts to deter them, including erecting low barriers around the carrots, growing the carrots between onions and spraying with garlic spray, but none have been very effective. The only way I've found to get clean carrots outside is to cover them over after sowing with insect-proof mesh to keep the flies off. It's a bit of a hassle, but worth it to get clean carrots. You also need to rotate the carrot bed every year because the pupae from the late-summer generation overwinter in the soil and emerge in spring. If you grow in the same spot, the emerging adults wake up to a ready food source whether you cover them or not!

insecticides available to control them. Nematodes can be watered into the soil and the microscopic nematodes will seek and kill the carrot fly larvae.

It's also said that sowing after late-May will avoid the first generation of larvae. Growing under a fine mesh such as **Enviromesh** acts as a physical barrier and prevents the flies laying eggs.

Below: Carrot root fly damage.

Sowing

In my polytunnel border and the veg plot, the seeds are sown thinly into shallow drills around 1.5cm-2cm (¾in) deep. Ground preparation should be as for parsnips and, remember, no fresh compost or manure!

It's important to sow the seed thinly along the rows to minimise thinning later on.

Outside sowing can start in late March or early April. In the polytunnel I sow in February or as soon as the soil temperature reaches 7.5°C.

Early carrots, especially round or short-rooted varieties, can be sown in pots of compost in the greenhouse. I use a mix of half and half multipurpose and John Innes compost. The seed is scattered very thinly, covered over with a thin layer of compost and kept moist. Once the seedlings are large enough to handle, thin them 2.5cm (1in) apart and let them grow on for a crop of early carrots.

Varieties

There are several types of carrot that you can grow and not all of them are orange! For early crops, sow Amsterdam and Nante types.

'Amsterdam Forcing 3' – An early carrot that can be sown early under cover, in containers or outside in the garden.

'Early Nante 5' – Also ideal for early sowing and for succession sowings outside.

'Resistafly F1' – One of several types that are less susceptible to carrot fly attack, but not in my garden, apparently!

'Paris Market 5' – A ball-rooted variety ideal for shallow soils or growing in containers.

'Autumn King' – An old variety that is hardy and produces large roots.

'Harlequin' – A mix of orange, purple, yellow and white roots for something a little different.

Left: To prevent root fly damage, grow carrots under mesh.

Growing and aftercare

In dry weather, keep carrots watered, but don't overdo it as too much water encourages masses of leaf growth. The seedlings will need to be thinned out when they are large enough to handle. Carefully pull out the seedlings, leaving a strong seedling every 2.5cm (1in) along the row. If you want large carrots, double the spacing or, in several weeks as the carrots grow, pull out every other one as baby carrots and leave the others to grow.

I can't stress enough the risk of carrot root fly and if the plants are growing under a mesh, re-cover them immediately after thinning as it's the scent of the carrot leaves that attracts the flies. I've often wondered if wearing a strong aftershave while thinning the carrots might keep the flies away!

Harvesting

Carrots can be pulled at any stage of growth and small, baby carrots are very sweet. They can, of course, be left to mature for use in the autumn and winter. Carrots are not as hardy as parsnips and if being left in the ground, it's a good idea to mulch them over to protect the roots from hard frost.

Martin's tip

Lift carrots in October or early November and store in buckets of damp sand or freeze them. If left in the ground, they are more susceptible to carrot fly damage over winter.

Right: Freshly pulled carrots grown in pots.

Parsnips and carrots in the kitchen

Parsnips and carrots are my favourite root veg and are a staple in any stew or casserole I make and feature in most of our dinners in some shape or form over the winter months. Carrots are probably used more in the kitchen as a base in loads of dishes as a mirepoix (pronounced meerpwah!). Pasta sauces, soups and stocks, for instance, will use a mix of two parts onion and one part each of carrots and celery at the start of cooking.

However, a real feature in my freezer is always carrot and parsnip soup using all the last of the stored crops and this keeps us going well into the spring – a really welcoming lunch on a cold spring gardening day!

Parsnips

Roast parsnips, a bit burnt at the edges and crispy all over but sweet and tender inside – perfect! Of course, they can be steamed or simmered for about ten minutes until tender or mashed into your creamy potato, but I think roasted is my favourite way to serve them.

When they're fresh out of the garden at the beginning of the harvesting season, they don't really need peeling, just wash and serve whole. As they get older and woodier later on in the season, they should be peeled and maybe have the central core removed if it's become too tough to eat.

Jill's tip

Parsnips will keep in the fridge for quite a few days but if we've dug too many, then I cut them into bite-sized chunks and parboil them for a couple of minutes along with some cubes of potato. Drain and cool then pack them into a freezer bag to use for a quick roasted or pan-fried side dish. I know I've always got some ready to use, just toss in some oil, season and roast for half an hour or so until golden brown.

Opposite page:
Top: Root veg bake.
Bottom: Sweet and sticky roast parsnips.

Parsnip cake

There are loads of carrot cake recipes around so for a change here's a parsnip cake to try. This cake is one that I've taken with me to our 'Gardening on the Menu' talks. It becomes a bit of a challenge to see if you can taste the parsnip! I don't think you can particularly, but the veg content in cakes always helps them to last longer and stay moist.

Cuts into 15 good-sized pieces
Takes about an hour plus cooling time

Ingredients

200g butter, melted
300g parsnips, grated (I've added in a carrot or you could add some grated squash or even apple)
140g sultanas
4 clementines or 2 oranges, zest and juice
300g self raising flour
Pinch of salt
300g soft light-brown sugar
2 good tsps mixed spice
1 tsp ginger or nutmeg
1 tsp bicarbonate of soda
4 large eggs, beaten
200g icing sugar
Scattering of granulated sugar or some crushed white sugar cubes

Method

- Grease and line a 30cm x 20cm tray-bake tin.
- Preheat oven to 180°C (fan 160°C), gas 4.
- Put the sultanas in a small bowl and add the clementine juice and zest from 2 fruits. Pop in the microwave and cook for 2 minutes on the high setting. Stir well and leave to cool.
- In a large bowl, sieve together the flour, sugar, spices, bicarb and salt.
- Melt the butter in a large bowl and leave to cool a little. Add in the beaten eggs and the sultanas along with any juices from the bowl and mix well together.
- Tip the buttery fruit mix into the dry ingredients and mix together with a wooden spoon.
- Add in the grated parsnip and give another good stir but don't overwork the batter.
- Pour into your baking tin then pop in the oven for a good 35–40 minutes. Test to

see if it's ready with a skewer poked into the middle of the cake - if it comes out clean, the cake's ready.

- Leave to cool in the tin then turn out onto a wire rack, ready for icing.
- Sift the icing sugar into a small bowl then stir in the zest from the remaining 2 clementines. Add the juice of 1 of the fruits and stir well. Add more juice a bit at a time to make a fairly runny icing.
- You can either drizzle or spread the icing over the cake, depending on the finish you prefer - either way, let it run down the sides a bit then scatter over the sugar.

This is one of those handy cakes that will keep for quite a few days so there's no rush to eat it unless, of course, you want to!

Perfect with a good strong cup of Yorkshire tea!

Easy cook – Parsnip dauphinoise

This is an easy side dish that makes a change from potatoes and can be prepared ahead.

- Slice a couple of parsnips very thinly and pop in a pan of boiling water for just 4 or 5 minutes.
- Pile into a greased, shallow ovenproof dish, season with salt and pepper and a sprinkling of nutmeg, and toss to coat.
- Pour over enough crème fraiche (about a 200ml tub) to coat, then scatter over a good handful of Parmesan.
- Pop in the oven, 190°C (fan 170°C), gas 5, for about 30 minutes until the top is golden.

Quick ideas for roasting

This is a great tip that I found in a James Martin book. It's become a firm favourite at Christmas. Mix equal amounts of sherry and runny honey together in a bowl along with some salt and pepper - for a couple of parsnips, use about 3 tablespoons of each. Add in your quartered parsnips and coat well. Tip everything into a roasting tray - there should be plenty of sticky liquid in the pan. Roast in the oven, 200°C (fan 180°C), gas 6, for about 30 minutes. The sherry evaporates and leaves a gorgeous sticky coating. Make sure you turn the parsnips a few times until they are golden brown and tender.

Alternatively, you could toss them in some olive oil and add in a good squeeze of maple syrup, or roast as normal then scatter over some grated Parmesan cheese for the last 10 minutes.

Carrots

It's a bit of a standing joke with our neighbours and good friends Linda and Del that they grow better carrots than us – it's true, although Martin is loath to admit it! Linda grows hers in a raised bed and is never bothered with root fly. If the root fly has taken hold of our crop then I sometimes go raiding her crop next door!

Raw, steamed, boiled, roasted or in soup or cakes, I love them. Baby carrots have to be my favourite – they just get trimmed and washed then straight into the pan for a light boiling. As they get older, they need to be peeled but I try not to peel too thickly as the most nutrients are supposed to be just under the skin.

Root veg bake

This is a dish that we've been having for years and it's a staple at our Christmas meal. It can be made ahead and frozen, and is a vital ingredient in our bubble and squeak on Boxing Day.

I always make a large amount so I've plenty left over – this recipe will serve 10 generously when served with other veg and leaves some spare to use the next day.

Takes about an hour

Ingredients

1.3kg mix of mostly carrots and parsnips with a bit of swede thrown in, cut into even-sized chunks
142ml tub soured cream
2 good tblsps horseradish sauce
A good tblsp of fresh thyme leaves

Top: Root veg bake - carrots and parsnips, mixed with sour cream and thyme.
Centre: the final dish. Any leftovers, can be added to vegetables for Martin's bubble and squeak.
Bottom: Bubble and squeak patties, browning nicely!

For the top:

50g butter
1 medium onion, finely chopped
50g white breadcrumbs
A handful of thyme leaves
25g Parmesan cheese, grated

Method

- Put the parsnip, carrot and swede into a large pan of boiling water, cover and cook for about 20 minutes until tender. Drain really well then mash together until fairly smooth - leave a few lumpy bits!
- Stir in the soured cream, horseradish and thyme and season well with salt and pepper.
- Spoon into a large ovenproof dish and put to one side.
- For the topping, melt the butter in a frying pan and cook the onion until golden brown.
- Tip in the breadcrumbs and stir until they are crisp and brown.
- Add the thyme and then scatter over the veg to roughly cover.
- Sprinkle the cheese over the top.
- Bake for 25–30 minutes at 190°C (fan 170°C), gas 5, until golden brown.

If making this ahead, then cool uncooked, cover and keep in the fridge or freezer. (If cooking from cold, give another 10 minutes in the oven.)

Quick cook - salad

Try a salad of carrot and apple cut into slices then tossed in a honey mustard dressing with some walnuts added on the top.

Martin's bubble and squeak

Martin's in charge of Boxing Day in our house. Our grown-up children are all guaranteed to come over for some of Dad's bubble and squeak, so I just sit back with a glass of something and let them do all the work!

We always use the root veg bake in it as it adds some extra flavours without any extra work. He's perfected his technique over the years and likes to think that this is the ultimate recipe!

Enough for 2

Takes about 20 minutes

Ingredients

All these ingredients are approximate, giving a generous-sized portion

2 tblsps mashed potato
2 tblsps root veg bake
2 heaped tblsps of roughly chopped cooked veg (whatever is left over)
1 small egg, beaten (Martin's secret ingredient!)
Salt and pepper

Method

- With a fork, mix together the potato, bake and veg, season, then mix in the egg to bind.
- Make into patties about 3cm–4cm thick.
- Melt a good glug of oil in a frying pan and cook without the patties touching on a medium heat for about 10 minutes.
- Turn carefully then cook for a further 5–8 minutes until warmed through and golden brown.
- Enjoy with cold meats, pork pie and a good spoonful of cranberry sauce.

Jill's tip

I like to roast carrots as well as parsnips. Keep them fairly chunky, probably cut in half across then halve the top end of the carrot lengthways. I usually parboil them first just for 3 or 4 minutes then toss in oil and any flavourings you fancy – maybe some thyme or a spice mix or add some red onion wedges. For a caramelised finish, you could add a sprinkling of brown sugar then roast in a fairly hot oven, 200°C (fan 180°C), gas 6, for about 15 minutes then turn and leave for another 5 minutes to finish browning. Add a bit more oil if they start to look dry.

Peppers and chillies in the garden

Capsicums in the form of sweet peppers and hot chilli peppers have become increasingly popular over recent years and for many, the hotter the better! We enjoy sweet peppers, but are not fans of the very hot chillies that blow your head off, although Jill does use some in moderation in several of her dishes.

Peppers are normally grown under cover for protection, but they can also be grown outside during the summer in a warm spot on a patio where they look very attractive when in fruit. The main advantage of growing your own is the huge choice of varieties that come in all shapes, colours and sizes - not to mention tastes!

Soil and conditions for growing

A sunny position is essential for the fruits to develop and ripen and if growing in the greenhouse border, the soil should be fertile and well drained.

I, however, always prefer to grow peppers in large pots. I find that restricting the roots slightly encourages better fruiting and it also means that you can move the plants around easily. You may want to stand them outside in hot weather, or move them into a warmer position when it starts to cool in autumn, and a pot gives you this flexibility.

For growing in pots, I use a good-quality multipurpose compost which is fine as long as you feed regularly through the growing season.

Varieties

Due to the huge popularity of sweet and chilli peppers, seed companies now sell a varied selection to choose from, ranging from very mild flavours to extremely hot ones – be warned!

Sweet pepper **'California Wonder Mixed'** – An old variety, but reliable, and will produce blocky fruits that turn from green to red, orange or yellow.

Sweet **pepper 'Corno di Toro Rosso'** – Produces long fruits up to 20cm (8in) long that ripen to red. Ideal in salads or on the barbecue.

Sowing and planting

Seeds need to be sown inside at a temperature of around 18°C-21°C. You can sow as early as early February, but remember that once the seeds have germinated, they need to be grown on in a light, warm place. I usually sow in early March which produces strong plants for May to grow on in a cold greenhouse or polytunnel. The seeds are sown in small pots of compost, covered with a thin layer of compost or vermiculite and watered in, before being put into the propagator.

Seedlings are pricked out into 9cm (3.5in) pots and grown on in the warm greenhouse until they are around 15cm-20cm (6in-8in) tall and have a good root system. At this point I pot into the final container which is around 25cm (10in) in diameter.

Pepper plants are available from garden centres in spring to grow on and these are perfect if you don't want to grow from seed, but the range of varieties is much smaller.

Sweet pepper '**Mini Bell**' – An improved mixture that produces small, blocky red or yellow fruits that are great in salads or for stuffing.

Chilli pepper '**Ring of Fire**' – Green fruits that ripen to red and, as its name suggests, it's hot.

Chill pepper '**Fish**' – I grow this one because of its name but also because it has attractive variegated leaves and small striped fruits that ripen to red. Medium to hot fruits.

Chilli pepper '**Scotch Bonnet**' – One to grow if you like very hot chillies. I've grown it once, but it's too hot for me!

Left: Sowing chilli seeds into pots.

Martin's tip

To prevent pot-grown plants from drying out in hot weather, stand them in a tray and add an inch or two of water to the tray each day for the plants to drink up through the drainage holes. Don't, however, allow the plant to stand in water permanently.

Top: Pepper plants in trays for watering and feeding.
Centre: Mixing up a high potash liquid fertiliser for peppers, tomatoes and cucumbers.
Bottom: Picking peppers whilst green for eating.

Above: Using a cane to support a pepper plant.

Left from top: Young peppers being protected from whitefly with yellow sticky traps.
Centre: '**Mini Bell**' sweet peppers.
Bottom: Chilli pepper '**Fish**'.

Aftercare

Always keep the plants moist and in good light. Peppers tend to be self-branching and will naturally make side shoots and a bushy plant, which is what we want. When flowering starts, feed weekly with a high-potash fertiliser to encourage the fruits to develop.

As the fruits grow and swell in size, the plants can get a little top heavy, so insert a cane or two down through the plant into the compost for support and to prevent branches from snapping off.

If the plants are kept in warm, light conditions such as a greenhouse or conservatory, they will often carry on growing and fruiting through autumn and into winter.

Harvesting and storing

The fruits of all peppers can be eaten at any stage of growth and they don't need to fully ripen to a colour. We start to pick while the fruits are still green and then in late summer we allow some to ripen to red or yellow, depending on the variety. By picking some green, immature fruit, the plant will produce a heavier crop overall.

Sweet peppers can be stored in a fridge for a few weeks. Chilli peppers, when ripe, can be dried or powdered for use over the winter.

Pests and diseases

Aphids – **Greenfly** on the new growth can be a problem, but they can easily be controlled by simply rubbing them off between your finger and thumb, or use an approved insecticide.

Whitefly – Can be a serious problem if not controlled. I hang yellow sticky traps between the plants to catch all flying insects and they work well. Alternatively, you can spray the plants with a suitable insecticide.

Botrytis – A fungal disease often called 'grey mould' that tends to be a problem in damp, cool growing conditions, either in spring or autumn. There are no fungicides to treat it and the best way to avoid it is to make sure the plants are well ventilated and not too close together. If a few leaves do develop the grey mould, pick them off and dispose of them.

Root rots – Can be a problem if the plants are grown in the same soil for many years. There are several fungal diseases that attack the roots, causing the plants to wilt. To avoid it, grow in fresh soil or in pots of compost.

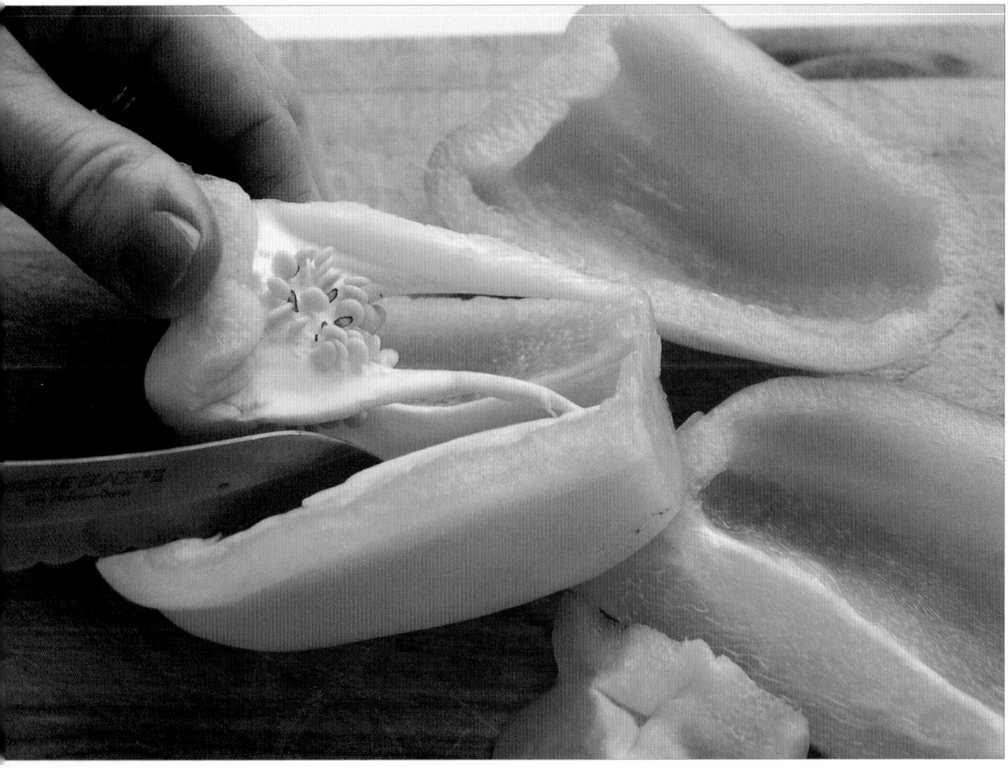

Peppers and chillies in the kitchen

You only have to look at a dish of peppers to feel that summer's well and truly here. I love seeing them ripen in the greenhouse alongside the tomatoes, cucumbers and aubergines. It makes me think of summer holidays on little Greek islands!

There's a huge range of tastes, from fiery hot chillies to sweet juicy orange peppers, and a huge range of uses in the kitchen. Stir fries, barbecues, salads, pasta sauces or casseroles, there's one to suit all requirements. Endlessly versatile, they can be stuffed, fried, griddled or roasted!

Of course, they don't suit everyone – Martin, for one, has a problem eating too many peppers as they can be hard to digest. It's the fibrous skins that cause the problem and green peppers are the worst as they are essentially unripe fruits. Fortunately, this is easily remedied by skinning peppers before eating.

Jill's tips

- However you're enjoying your peppers, make sure that you remove all the core, pith and seeds before eating. They are bitter and will really affect the flavour of any dish. If they are for general use and for chopping, then I tend to cut down from the stalk, avoiding the core, so that I end up with big slabs of pepper that I can chop or dice as required.
- Make skinning easy – cut your peppers in half and remove the seeds and stalk. Put under a hot grill, skin side up, and leave until the peppers are blistered and looking quite burnt. Carefully remove and put into a freezer bag. Leave some air in the bag and seal, then rest for about ten minutes. The skins will peel away really easily, leaving softened, partly cooked peppers. If there are some juices in the bag, don't waste them but dip a bit of bread in and treat yourself!
- If I do more than I need, then they store well in the fridge in a little olive oil.

Top and centre: Mediterranean chutney - finely chopped vegetables before sugar, vinegar and spices are added.
Bottom: Test for set before potting up.

Mediterranean chutney

This is a fabulous, spicy chutney that you can make in September and squirrel away for Christmas as it goes really well with cold meats and pork pie. I often include a jar of this in Christmas hampers!

Makes about 6 x 370ml (1lb) jars

Takes about 3 hours – or less if someone will help with the chopping!

Ingredients

6 peppers, mixed colours but only 2 green, flesh chopped small
1–2 chillies, finely chopped (depending on how hot you like it)
1.35kg tomatoes, skinned and chopped
2 small aubergines or 4 small courgettes, chopped small
1.5kg onions, finely chopped
6 cloves garlic, crushed
525g soft brown sugar
450ml white wine vinegar
1½ tblsps salt
1½ tblsps coriander seeds, crushed
1½ tblsps paprika (smoked works well)
2 tsp cayenne (optional if you like a little heat)
Sterilised jars with screw-top lids
Saucer in the freezer

Method

› Put all the chopped ingredients and the garlic into a large, lidded pan. Bring to a gentle simmer then cover and cook for about an hour until tender, stirring now and again.

› Ideally, transfer into a preserving pan and add the sugar, vinegar, salt and spices. Stir over a low heat until the sugar has dissolved.

› Turn up the heat and bring to a bubble, then cook for about 40–50 minutes until the watery liquid has evaporated and the chutney looks much thicker. Make sure you stir the chutney quite a lot near the end of the cooking time as it will catch on the bottom of the pan as it thickens. When you stir through the chutney, it should leave a trail in the pan. Try my chilled saucer test – put a spoonful on a frozen saucer and run your finger through it. If it leaves a clear path, then the chutney is ready.

› Spoon out or carefully pour into your jars, up to the brim, and pop the lids on straight away.

This is a chutney that does need to mature to taste its best – ideally at least three months. I found a forgotten jar of this at the back of my store cupboard.

Jill's chilli tips

- Capsaicin is the heat maker in a chilli and it's mainly found in the pith and seeds, so remove before slicing if you want a milder flavour.
- If you do overdo it, then try milk or yoghurt rather than water to cool you down.
- Always remember to wash your hands after working with chillies in the kitchen - never rub your eyes or nip to the loo first!

It was fourteen months old but trust me, it only improves with age!

Easy no cook – chilli powder

If you have time and an airing cupboard, then dry your chillies to use throughout the year. I like to dry them slowly on wire racks, turning and checking on them now and again.

You could make your own chilli powder and keep in your spice drawer - blitz your dried chillies in a liquidiser and store in jars in a cool, dark place or make a ready-to-use mix for chilli con carne.

Use a teaspoon of chilli powder and add:

2 tblsps paprika
3 tsps dried oregano
2 tsps cumin
2 tsps garlic powder
Simply put everything in your jar, seal and shake together.

Chilli jam

We love this tasty condiment that adds a touch of heat to your food. You can regulate the heat by the type of chillies you use - generally the smaller the type, the hotter they'll be!

We like to add it as a topping to some cheese on toast, or you can add a spoonful to a pasta sauce or use as a dipping sauce for some fresh king prawns.

This quantity makes approximately 1 x 450g (1lb) jar but as you only eat a little at a time, I like to pot it into several smaller jars. You can easily double up the ingredients but allow about 10 minutes extra simmering time.

Takes about an hour

Ingredients

4 red chillies (remember - the smaller the chillies, the hotter the jam!)
2 large red peppers
2 medium tomatoes
4 cloves garlic, finely chopped
300g golden caster sugar (or demerara sugar)
100ml red wine vinegar
Chunk of fresh root ginger
Juice of 1 lime

Top and centre: Chilli jam - chillies, tomatoes, red peppers and garlic are chopped, then blended. Once boiled, the ginger pieces are removed and lime juice added.
Bottom: Potting up - fill to just below brim of jar and seal immediately.

Sterilised jars with screw-top lids

Method

- Cut the stalks from the chillies and chop roughly, leaving the seeds in.
- Roughly chop the tomatoes, leaving the seeds in (it helps the jam to set) and chop the peppers without the seeds.
- Put all of the chopped ingredients into a blender. Blitz until puréed.
- Put the purée into your preserving pan and add the sugar and the red wine vinegar. Peel the lump of ginger and add, whole, to the mix.
- Bring to the boil, stirring all the time, then turn the heat down and simmer gently for about 30–40 minutes, stirring now and again. A foamy scum will come to the surface - leave for about 10 minutes then just skim it off and discard.
- The jam will change in appearance and texture - it thickens and gets quite sticky and shiny. It will also have changed to a much deeper red colour.
- Leave on the heat, remove the ginger and stir in the lime juice - it helps the jam to thicken a little.
- Pot up into your warm jars - to just below the brim - and put the lids on immediately.
- As the jam cools, it will thicken a little more but it should still be slightly runny.

Each batch I make is a different heat, so I usually put a guide on the label - 'quite hot' or 'fairly hot', or draw some chillies (the more chillies, the hotter the jam!).

Jill's tip - freezing chillies

As we always get a glut of chillies, I freeze them – I slice them first then put portion-sized amounts in pieces of cling film and wrap well. These all go in a freezer bag ready to use when needed.

If I'm feeling very organised, then I make a spice mix and add some garlic and ginger into chopped chilli, then freeze. They're really easy to use later in curries, sauces and stews when I need them.

Tomatoes in the garden

I've grown tomatoes since I was a teenager and I still look forward to sowing the seed every spring with the promise of delicious ripe fruits in the summer and early autumn. Home-grown tomatoes are wonderful and bear no comparison to supermarket tomatoes. For a start, when growing your own you can choose the variety that you like and you can allow them to fully ripen on the plant before you pick them, warmed by the sun. I think there's no excuse for not growing your own tomatoes and even if you have limited space, they can be grown in containers and hanging baskets.

We grow ours mainly under cover in the greenhouse or polytunnel where the added protection helps with growth and ripening. If you can provide a sunny, sheltered spot in the garden, many types can also be grown outside with success, especially if you grow blight-resistant varieties.

Growing conditions

There's no doubt about it that to grow well, tomatoes need warmth, hence the reason most are grown under cover.

They can be grown in the greenhouse borders, large pots or growbags and some people also use a hydroponic system, although I haven't grown them this way myself.

My preferred method is to grow them directly in the soil where they can get their roots down and make strong plants. However, if you grow in the same soil each year, root rots and diseases can be a problem. To overcome this, I alternate the polytunnel borders to give the soil a rest for a year and so far, so good!

I also make sure the soil is in good condition and in early spring I work in plenty of garden compost to enrich the soil and feed weekly through the summer.

Varieties

The choice of tomatoes is huge and seed catalogues list lots of different types, from cherry tomatoes to large beefsteak. When I first started growing tomatoes, it was varieties such as '**Moneymaker**', '**Ailsa Craig**', '**Gardener's Delight**' and '**Alicante**'. These are all still available and are good to grow, but there are so many new varieties with excellent flavours and many also have good disease resistance. We like to grow a mixture of different shapes, sizes and colours to add variety to the salad bowl and all have their individual taste. Here are just some

My second choice would be to grow the tomatoes in large pots of good-quality potting compost. The pot needs to be at least 10 litres in size, otherwise they dry out too quickly. When grown this way, you can get some excellent results as long as you water and feed regularly. As for grow bags, I don't really like them as they are too shallow and dry out very quickly.

Sowing seed and pricking out

Tomatoes are easy to grow from seed and if you don't have a greenhouse propagator, they can be raised on a windowsill. To germinate, the seed needs a temperature of around 21°C. At this temperature, seedlings should emerge in five to seven days. Any cooler and germination will be longer. I sow the seed thinly in a small pot filled with multipurpose compost that has been lightly firmed down. Cover with a thin layer of sieved compost or vermiculite until you can't see the seeds, gently water the compost and keep warm.

Once the seedlings have developed their two seed leaves, prick them out into small, individual pots to grow on. I use 9cm (3.5in) pots filled with multipurpose compost. Make a hole in the compost and carefully transplant the seedling so that the seed leaves are just above the compost level. Keep them moist and grow on in a light, warm position, but not too hot otherwise the plants will grow tall and leggy. A frost-free greenhouse or cool windowsill is fine.

The time to sow the seeds will depend on where and how you are growing on the plants. If you intend to grow them in a heated greenhouse,

that we've grown over the past few years with good results.

'Shirley F1' – Still regarded as one of the best tomatoes that produces medium-sized fruits. It's easy to grow and has good disease resistance.

'Akron F1' – A superb tomato that produces a heavy crop of good-sized, tasty fruits well into autumn.

'Red Bodyguard F1' – The fruits ripen to deep red and are very fleshy with an excellent flavour.

'Crimson Crush F1' – Can be grown under cover or outside where it produces a heavy crop of fruit. It also has very good blight resistance.

'Indigo Rose' – A black tomato that produces medium-sized fruit that are very high in antioxidants and has a lovely flavour.

Martin's tip

If you are sowing more than one type of tomato, label the pot as you sow as it's very easy to mix up the seedlings!

'Santonio F1' – This is a lovely cherry tomato that produces long trusses of cherry-plum fruits.

'Rainbow Blend F1' – A mixture of baby plum fruits in yellow, orange and red that are great in salads or for roasting.

'Tumbling Tom' – A naturally trailing tomato that is ideal for growing in hanging baskets and containers outside, producing masses of small cherry fruits.

'Firecracker' – A compact, trailing variety that produces red plum fruits with yellow stripes that is ideal for a hanging basket or container outside.

'Big Daddy F1' – A beefsteak variety with large red, fleshy fruits that taste wonderful.

Top: Sowing tomato seeds.
Centre: Pricking out seedlings.
Bottom: Potting a young tomato plant into a larger pot

Top: Young tomato plants ready for planting in the greenhouse.
Centre: Planting into the greenhouse border.
Bottom: Alternatively, you can grow tomatoes in large pots.

seed can be sown as early as February. For planting out in a cold greenhouse or polytunnel, sow in March. For outdoor plants, sowing can wait until early April. I allow around six to eight weeks from sowing to produce a plant ready for planting out but this, of course, varies depending on the time of the year and temperatures.

Growing on and aftercare

The ideal time to plant out into the soil border or large container is when the young tomato plant is approximately 20cm (8in) tall and when the first flower buds have formed in the top of the plant. If you are buying tomato plants from a nursery, choose those that have a good green colour and are not drawn or leggy.

In late spring, it is important to protect the plants from late frosts, so even in a greenhouse it is worth covering over the plants with fleece on frosty nights. Don't worry too much if the plant takes on a purple tinge, this is caused by a few cool nights. The plants usually recover as the weather warms up and grow away strongly.

Vine tomatoes grown as a single stem will need to be supported. This can be done with tall bamboo canes to which the stem is tied with string at regular intervals. Alternatively, a strong string line suspended down from the greenhouse frame and tied around the base of the plant can be used. As the plant grows, it can be twisted around the string.

Watering and feeding is vital for a healthy crop. The plants should never be allowed to dry out, but at the same time the compost should not be waterlogged. I'm often asked how much water to give a tomato plant each day, but I'm afraid there is no simple answer. The amount

Pests and diseases

Tomatoes can have their fair share of problems, but if grown well, watered and fed regularly, they are often trouble free, so don't be put off by potential problems!

Tomato blight – Mainly a problem on outdoor tomatoes, but can also affect greenhouse plants. The foliage quickly develops brown patches and dies back. No sprays are available for blight, but there are now several varieties available that show good resistance to the disease.

Whitefly – Probably the most common pest to afflict tomatoes. If not controlled, it will weaken the plants and the fruits will develop black, sooty mould on them. If spotted, control the whiteflies by hanging yellow sticky traps between the plants or spray with a suitable insecticide.

will depend on the temperature and size of pot the plants are growing in. Remember, small pots dry out very quickly in hot weather. The secret is to check the plants daily and keep the compost or soil constantly moist, but not soggy. Irregular watering will cause blossom end rot, tough skins and split fruits.

Feeding starts once the first flower truss has opened and tiny fruits have started to set. From this point I feed weekly with high-potash fertiliser or tomato feed to make sure the plants have all the nutrients they need for healthy growth.

To help with pollination, tap the plants to disperse the pollen or spray in the evening or early morning with water to increase humidity which helps the pollen to flow.

Also remember to ventilate on warm days to prevent the plants from overheating and to allow pollinating insects into the greenhouse.

Side shoots growing between the main stem and leaf stalk also need to be removed on a regular basis, otherwise what is intended as a single stem will very quickly become a large, unruly plant! Simply snap out the side shoots with your finger and thumb. If you are growing bush or trailing types, do not remove side shoots.

Opposite:
Top left: Tie in a tomato plant to a cane with soft string.
Right: Pinching out side shoots.
Bottom left: Jill removing the growing point to stop growth.
Right: Healthy tomato plants in the poly tunnel.

Foot and root rots – There are several fungal diseases such as verticillium and fusarium that can cause plants to wilt as a result of the roots or water-carrying cells in the stem being damaged. There are no treatments available for these diseases. Always grow in clean pots and use new compost. If growing in the soil, rotate the crops each year and avoid over-watering.

Fern-like foliage – Occasionally tomato leaves become twisted and distorted and develop fern-like leaves. This is usually due to weedkiller contamination. It only takes a minute amount of weedkiller, often lawn weedkiller drifting in the air, to cause the damage or in some cases it is caused by using contaminated compost. If this happens, there is nothing you can do other than dispose of the plant and be extra careful if treating your lawn.

Magnesium deficiency – Can occur from mid-summer when the plant is carrying a heavy crop of fruit. The leaves turn yellow between the veins, starting low down on

Once the plants reach the top of the cane or when they have produced six or seven trusses of fruit, pinch out the growing point to divert energy to the developing and ripening fruits. With plants growing outside, this is usually done after four to five trusses. Although it's tempting to let the plants carry on growing and producing trusses, fruits setting late in the season don't always have time to fully develop and ripen before autumn.

Once the lower trusses are fully formed and starting to change colour, you can start to remove a few of the lower leaves, again to divert energy to the fruits. However, green leaves produce food for the plants, so don't remove too many leaves too early. When the leaves start to yellow, though, they can be snapped off from the main stem. This improves ventilation around the fruits which helps with the ripening process. Later in the season when all the fruits are starting to turn from green to orange, more foliage can be removed up the stem.

Martin's tip

On hot days, damp down the greenhouse path with water to cool the temperature and increase humidity for better growth.

the plant and working upwards. Regular feeding with tomato fertiliser can be the cause, as the high levels of potash lock away the magnesium. To remedy the problem, spray the plants with Epsom salts at 100g in 5 litres of water a few times through the summer.

Blossom end rot – Very common and easy to recognise. The base of the fruits develop a black spot that enlarges as the fruits grow and ripen. It's caused by irregular watering which results in a calcium deficiency. Never allow the plants to dry out – water regularly.

Split fruits – This is usually caused by changeable growing conditions. Irregular watering and allowing the plants to dry out followed by lots of water often results in the skins splitting. Fluctuating temperatures also harden the skin and can cause areas of russeting.

Left, top: Attaching yellow sticky traps to catch whitefly.
Bottom: Damping down the path to increase humidity.
Above, right: Blossom end rot.
Bottom: Example of split fruit - a sign of irregular watering.

Harvesting

Tomatoes ripen from the bottom truss up and the ideal time to pick them is when they are ripe and showing a good colour. The fruits should be snapped off at the 'knuckle', just above the leafy calyx on top of the fruit. In a greenhouse or polytunnel, fruits will continue to ripen into early autumn, especially if the weather is mild. As the temperatures start to drop, cut back on watering and keep the soil or compost just moist. If the soil and atmosphere are too wet, it can lead to problems with fungal diseases and moulds. Close the greenhouse vents at night to seal in some warmth and if you can, use a fan to keep the air circulating as this also helps the last fruit of the season to ripen.

Fruits on plants growing outside will be damaged by autumn frost, so check the weather forecast and pick them if a frost is forecast and ripen them on a warm windowsill.

Tomatoes in hanging baskets

Trailing tomatoes such as '**Tumbling Tom**' are ideal for growing in pots or hanging baskets. They are very easy to look after and as long as you keep the compost well-watered and the plants fed weekly with a high-potash fertiliser, you should get masses of very tasty cherry tomatoes. There is no side shooting needed, but if the plants get too large, you can pinch back shoots to restrict growth, and any yellow foliage should be removed.

Right: The well named cherry tomato 'Gardener's Delight'. *Bottom:* The attractive fruit of 'Firecracker'.

Tomatoes in the kitchen

My favourite time of year in the polytunnel has to be tomato time! I wait and wait, willing them to turn red, and it seems to take forever at the start of the season. Friends in our garden club tell me they've been picking for weeks and I try not to be as green as my tomatoes, but then they start to turn and I am officially in seventh heaven! Of course, then they come thick and fast in all shapes, sizes and colours, but I love them all! I suppose if I had to pick a favourite, then it would have to be the beefsteak tomatoes.

The whole family loves tomatoes - our old Labrador, Ellie, was quite partial to them. She'd graze on a few of the lower trusses, splattering tomato juice all over her face! When the children were little, they would wander into the greenhouse and pick cherry tomatoes like sweets, especially the little yellow 'Sungold' ones.

Quick no cook – Tomato salsa

Serves 4 as a dip
Takes 10 minutes

Peel, de-seed and finely chop a couple of large tomatoes then pop in a bowl along with half a red onion and half a green chilli, both finely diced. Mix together with a good handful of chopped fresh coriander and the juice of about half a lime along with a good pinch of caster sugar.

Leave for about half an hour to let the flavours mingle but serve within a couple of hours of making.

This is great for serving as a dip with crisps or sticks of raw vegetables. Alternatively, toast some thin slices of ciabatta on both sides, rub over with a garlic clove to leave some flavour then drizzle with olive oil. Pile on some salsa and serve as a light bite.

Jill's tip

To skin tomatoes, simply pop them in a large bowl and pour boiling water over them. Leave for a couple of minutes, piercing them with a sharp knife if the skins don't burst straight away. Drain, then you should find that the skins have split and will peel away really easily. The riper they are, the quicker it will happen.

Tomato rice salad

You can't beat a rice salad as an accompaniment for loads of summer dishes and if we do get some sunny weather, this is easy to throw together for a barbecue with friends.

Serves 4–6

Takes about 45 minutes

Ingredients

Good glug of oil
1 onion, chopped small
4 cloves garlic, crushed
200g long grain white or brown rice
350ml vegetable stock

For the dressing:

3 tblsps white wine vinegar
4–5 sprigs of thyme, stalks removed
1 tsp runny honey
1 tsp Dijon mustard
80ml extra virgin olive oil
Salt and pepper

For the veg:

You can vary the salad veg you use – anything that's fresh, ripe and colourful

2 peppers, a mix of colours, de-seeded and chopped
½ red onion, finely chopped
½ cucumber, skinned and seeds removed, chopped
Good handful of tomatoes – mixed varieties (depending on size) skinned and chopped
2 small courgettes, chopped
2 tblsps chopped fresh parsley

For serving:

Handful of black olives, halved
25g flaked almonds, toasted

Method

- Heat the vegetable oil in a large, lidded frying pan and add the onion and half the garlic. Fry gently for about 5 minutes until softened. Add in the rice and stir to coat for a couple of minutes. Pour in the stock and season if your stock needs it. Stir then bring to a very gentle simmer, pop the lid on and leave to cook for 20 minutes. Turn off the heat, leaving the lid on, and leave for about 15 minutes. Take the lid off, stir with a fork to fluff up and leave for 5 minutes to cool a little.
- Whilst the rice is cooking, prepare the veg and the dressing: put the vinegar into a large bowl along with the thyme then whisk in the garlic, mustard and honey until well combined. Pour in a little of the olive oil at a time, whisking constantly. Put to one side.
- Combine the tomatoes, cucumber, peppers, onion, courgettes and parsley in a bowl ready to add to the salad.
- When the rice has cooled a little, tip it into the bowl containing the dressing (give it a little whisk first) and use a fork to coat and fluff it up.
- Add all the vegetables to the rice and mix together. Transfer to a serving bowl and scatter with the toasted almonds and the olives.

Slow-roasted cherry tomato sauce

We always grow two or three cherry tomato plants which give us plenty to eat and plenty to turn into this delicious sauce. Normally I'll mix all the varieties together for basic sauces and soups but there is a particular flavour to roasted cherry tomatoes that in the middle of winter is a real blast of summer flavour. I make a big batch and bottle it ready to use on pasta.

Makes about 500ml of sauce
Ready in about 35 minutes

Ingredients

700g cherry tomatoes
2–3 garlic cloves, very finely chopped
2 tblsps oil
1 tblsp balsamic vinegar

Method

- Use a sharp knife to put a cross in the top of each tomato - if they split when picked, then don't bother with the cross.
- In a large bowl, mix together the oil, vinegar and garlic. Tip in the tomatoes and toss to make sure everything is coated. Put in a single layer in a shallow ovenproof dish so that they are fairly tightly packed.
- Pop in the oven, 180°C (fan 160°C), gas 4, for about 30–40 minutes until the tomatoes are tender and are just starting to char at the edges and split open.
- Use a slotted spoon to put the tomatoes into a sieve. Push through to make a thick sauce, leaving the pips and skin behind. Don't forget to scrape the underside of the sieve when you've finished.
- Use the leftover juices in the dish to make it to the right consistency for you.
- (Cook's perk: dip some crusty bread into any leftover juices - they're unbelievably good!)

Quick cook – Tomato and mozzarella toasts

The slow-roasted cherry tomato sauce is so versatile and can be used thinned with stock and milk as soup or to top chicken, fish or pasta, but one of my favourite uses is to make a light snack on toast.

Drizzle some slices of bread (ciabatta works well) with olive oil and toast lightly on one side under a preheated grill. Spread some of the sauce over the untoasted side and scatter with some torn basil leaves. Top with some thin slices of mozzarella cheese then pop under the grill for a few minutes until melted and turning golden brown.

Jill's tip

To save for use over the winter, pour the hot slow-roasted cherry tomato sauce into warm, sterilised jars and seal with screw-top lids (not fully tightened) then carefully place in a large pan of boiling water. Ideally, sit them on a trivet or a tea towel in the bottom of the pan. The water should cover the lids. Simmer for about 20 minutes, which will ensure they will last the winter through without going mouldy. Remove from the water, tighten the lids well then leave to cool before storing in a cool, dark cupboard. The lids may pop as they cool; don't panic, it shows that all the air has been sucked out.

Jill's tip

Many years ago, I had a holiday in Spain and after a long, hot walk in the hills came across a little restaurant where I had the most marvellous meal which was accompanied by rough wedges of huge, juicy tomatoes drizzled with olive oil. So simple, but perfect.
I learnt a huge lesson then and always try to serve tomatoes as simply as possible with just a drizzle of oil and balsamic vinegar and a grinding of sea salt. The secret, I think, is to leave it for about half an hour before eating, giving the tomatoes time to start releasing their juices and flavour.

Top: Remove the insides of the tomatoes
Centre: Mix your filling together
Bottom: Enjoy!

Greek-style stuffed beefsteak tomatoes

We love holidaying in the Greek islands and a dish I always look forward to is baked stuffed tomatoes. I've tried to replicate it at home and we enjoy these in the middle of summer, pretending that we're sitting in a little Greek tavern with the sea lapping on the shore!

Serves 2

Takes about half an hour

› Slice off the tops of a couple of large beefsteak tomatoes and scoop out the inside with a dessertspoon. Chop up and put in a bowl along with any juices, a crushed garlic clove and some salt and pepper.
› Add this to some warm, just-done couscous and fluff up with a fork – this is a great way of adding flavour to couscous.
› Lightly toast a handful of pine nuts in a dry frying pan then put into a small bowl with a handful of sultanas, a good glug of oil, a squeeze of lemon juice and a bit of zest, and some chopped herbs – marjoram and mint work well but you could use mint or basil. Mix this into the couscous.
› Spoon the filling into the tomatoes, pressing down firmly, and make a dome on top. Pop the tops back on, put on a baking tray and drizzle over some olive oil. Bake in the oven, 200°C (fan 180°C), gas 6, for about 20 minutes until the tomatoes are soft and gently tinged brown at the edges.
› We like to enjoy this on its own with a green salad and chunks of feta cheese but it also tastes really good with gammon.

Fruit

Apples in the garden

I've always enjoyed eating apples so I suppose it naturally follows that I enjoy growing them. Our small orchard was planted during our first winter at Thornycroft from trees I grafted from our old garden. I chose varieties that I like and have since added a few more, giving us a total of nineteen different cooking and dessert apples in the garden.

I grafted onto a dwarfing rootstock - M26 - as I didn't want huge trees that need a ladder to pick the fruits. My aim is to maintain the trees at a maximum of around 2.4m (8ft) so that the fruits can be picked from the ground, very important as Jill and I aren't very tall!

Most of our trees are grown with a short trunk and a head of branches on top, but we also have a few trained apples in the form of step-overs and upright cordons in the garden.

Several years on, the trees have all established well and we now get an awful lot of fruit. In hindsight, maybe eight or ten trees would have been enough, but I like to grow a variety and each fruit has its own distinct flavour. We eat lots of them fresh, but due to the volume of apples we get in a good year, we now juice some and, of course, Jill uses them in lots of delicious recipes. If the old saying, 'An apple a day keeps the doctor away,' is true, we've nothing to worry about!

Soil conditions

Apples will grow in most soils as long as the drainage is fairly good. Although the rootstock will determine the overall size of the tree, the soil type also plays an important role. For example, the same tree planted on a light, sandy soil will not grow as well as one in a good, fertile loam that holds on to moisture and nutrients.

In our garden the soil is good, so to prevent excessive growth I allow the grass in the orchard to grow up to the base of the trees. This gives some competition to the trees and

Varieties

The choice of apple varieties is huge, but here are a few that we grow successfully in our garden. When choosing apples, bear in mind that they need a pollinator, which is basically another variety of apple tree that is nearby and in flower at the same time. Catalogues will have details of which pollinating group the various trees are in.

also helps to reduce the vigour a little more. However, when using dwarf rootstocks on poor, sandy soil, remove the grass in a circle around the trees to allow maximum water and nutrients to the tree roots.

Know your rootstocks before you choose your tree

All apples are grafted or budded onto a rootstock and this is what controls their vigour. A dwarf rootstock has small, weaker roots which results in a smaller tree, whereas a rootstock with strong growing roots will produce a large, vigorous tree. Although there are many rootstocks available, nurseries tend to use just three for garden trees. M9 is dwarfing and produces a tree around 2.4m–3.0m (8ft–10ft) tall which needs permanent staking because of its small root system. A semi-dwarf rootstock is M26 with slightly more vigour. It only needs staking for around four years and produces a tree around 3.0m-3.6m (10ft-12ft) tall. M106 is semi-vigorous and grows to 3.6m–5.0m (12ft–16ft) and is ideal where you want a slightly larger tree. However, as already mentioned, soil types, growing conditions and pruning also affect the size.

Planting

Traditionally, fruit trees are planted in autumn and winter and this is still true of bare-root trees. These are field grown young trees that are lifted in autumn when their leaves drop. Containerised fruit trees can, in theory, be planted all year round as the roots are not disturbed, but if planting when the tree is actively growing, you will need to water regularly.

Whatever time you plant, the important thing is to dig a large planting hole and break up any compacted layers in the base of the hole. If using a tree stake for support, this needs to be knocked into the hole before planting to avoid root damage.

Stand the tree in the hole, spread the roots and gradually backfill with soil, firming as you go. Plant to the existing soil mark on the trunk, making sure the graft (the knobbly bit) is above soil level. Finally, tie the tree to the stake and if the soil is dry, water in.

Tree shapes

Apple trees can be trained into several different shapes known as bush, standard, pyramid or spindle, but most people basically want a

'Discovery' – One of the earliest varieties that is ready from mid-August. A dessert apple with good flavour, but it needs eating quickly as it doesn't keep for long.

'Egremont Russet' – Dessert apple ready for picking in early October. Keeps well and has a distinctive nutty flavour and is lovely with Wensleydale cheese.

'Bramley's Seedling' – I might be a little biased, but I think this Nottinghamshire cooking apple is still the best. Pick in mid-October and use it through until the following spring.

'Katy' – A heavy cropping dessert apple that produces sweet, juicy apples and good flavour. Ready to pick in mid-September and will keep until the end of October.

'Ribston Pippin' – A very old Yorkshire eating apple that is a parent of 'Cox's Orange Pippin'. It has good flavour and is ready to harvest in October and keeps until January.

'Grandpa Buxton' – A fairly recent early season cooking apple from near Ripon in North Yorkshire with good flavour. Pick in September and use by Christmas.

'Newton Wonder' – A mid-season cooking apple that has a really lovely flavour. Harvest in October and use by December.

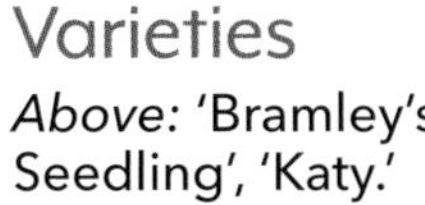

Varieties

Above: 'Bramley's Seedling', 'Katy.'

Right, top to bottom: 'Discovery', 'Ribston', 'Pippin', Grandpa Buxton, 'Red Love'.

Top: An old, established espalier apple tree.
Bottom: Summer pruning a trained step-over tree.

compact tree that isn't too tall. Pruning in the early stages determines the shape and the golden rule is to have an open centre for air flow and a framework of branches to form the shape. What we want are strong branches lower down that will carry the weight of the eventual crop and we get this by pruning back branches on the young tree to encourage side branches to develop. Books often say prune to a wine-glass shape, which helps to create the permanent framework.

Where growing space is limited or you want a more formal effect, apple trees can be bought in, or trained into, a variety of shapes, such as cordons, fans, espaliers or step-overs. These trained trees look very attractive and produce a good crop of fruit in a small space. Maintenance is also very simple and once the shape has been formed, all the pruning is done in the summer.

Pruning

Pruning can be done in winter or summer and in some cases both in order to maintain a compact tree.

Young trees need formative pruning to create the framework of branches and this can take two or three years. In winter, cut out the central, vertical stem down to a side branch. Ideally you want three or four side branches off the main trunk and these should be shortened by two-thirds to an outward facing bud. In the second winter the new branches that have grown should also be shortened by two-thirds, again to encourage more side branches the following year. By now the tree will be forming a well-branched shape to give you the traditional wine glass.

Established trees can be pruned in winter to cut out any weak, twiggy growth in the centre of the tree and to maintain its shape, but don't get carried away because the more you prune a tree back, the more it will grow the following year. Heavy pruning also cuts off the flowering wood, meaning little or no fruit the year after. With winter pruning the secret is little and often. Simply reduce any long, upright branches by up to two-thirds or to a horizontal growing branch. Cut out crossing branches that are rubbing each other

Martin's tip

When pruning, it pays to be able to identify the difference between fruit buds and growth buds. The rounder, fat buds are fruiting buds and will produce blossom in spring followed by fruit. Buds that are long and slender are growth buds ready to produce new shoots in springs.

and any dead wood. When finished, the basic tree shape should be the same, but just a little more open and tidier.

Summer pruning is to maintain a shape and to encourage fruiting spurs to form. These are very short stems on which flowers and fruit develop the following year. With established bush trees, long summer growths can be thinned or shortened to a few inches to create the spurs in August. This instantly tidies up the tree in late summer and diverts energy to the developing fruits on the tree.

On trained apple trees such as cordons, espaliers and step-overs, again cut back all the current season's growth to an inch or two to create spurs. This is also done in August and keeps the decorative shape of the tree.

Martin's tip

If you intend to grow trained apple trees, look for varieties that are 'spur' bearing as these produce blossom and fruit on the short growths. 'Tip' bearing varieties produce fruit on the tips of the previous season's shoots and do not respond to hard pruning in summer as it basically cuts off the fruit buds.

Left: Reducing long side shoots to form a good shape on a young tree.

Codling moth – This is what causes maggots in the core of the fruits in late summer. The small brown moth lays her eggs on the developing fruits from late spring and they burrow into the fruits and cause damage. To control with sprays is difficult, but I find that using pheromone traps work very well as prevention rather than cure. The traps are hung in the trees at the end of May and they attract and catch the male moths, hopefully before they mate with females. Although not 100% effective, they greatly reduce the damage.

Woolly aphids – This aphid, unlike others, feeds by sucking sap through the bark and the grey/white clusters are easy to spot along branches. For protection they cover themselves in a white waxy substance, making it difficult to control them. Some insecticides can be used on apples or, where there are only a few, wash them off with a strong jet of water. A winter wash will also help, as long as you direct the spray into all the nooks and crannies where the aphids will be over-wintering.

Pests and diseases

I could write a book on pests and diseases of apples, but that might put you off growing them, so I've only listed the main problems. And, unfortunately, apples do have their fair share of problems!

Commercially grown fruits undergo a regime of spraying to kill pests and diseases. In the garden, it's possible to grow decent fruits without having to spray, as long as you don't mind the odd blemish or grub! In many cases, keeping the trees well pruned and maintaining good garden hygiene will help to reduce disease problems. This means picking up and disposing of any diseased leaves or fruits to prevent spread. A winter wash using natural plant oils on the bare branches also helps to control hibernating pests and eggs.

Very few sprays are available to gardeners, but a product that is used by many is **Plant Invigorator** which contains a blend of surfactants (plant wash) and nutrients. It is safe and cleared for use on edible crops where it helps to control many pests and diseases.

Opposite page
Top: Winter wash fruit trees in the dormant season to kill overwintering insects and eggs.
Centre: Hanging a codling moth trap.
Bottom: Woolly aphid on an apple tree.

Canker – Apple canker is caused by a fungus that kills areas of the bark, creating sunken, dead patches. Sometimes the canker girdles a branch, causing it to die. It is often worse in trees growing in heavy clay or waterlogged soils, so always try to improve the drainage before planting. No treatments are available. Where cankers develop on small branches, cut the damaged wood out and treat the area with a wound paint to seal the cut.

Above: Apple canker.

Martin's tip

If a heavy crop of apples develop in spring, it's a good idea to thin the fruits after the natural drop in early summer known as the June drop (this tends to be July in North Yorkshire!) First remove the central fruit known as the 'King' fruit as this is often mis-shapen, then thin cookers to one or two fruits per cluster and desserts to two or three to allow the fruits more room to develop.

Above: Brown rot.

Left, Top: Thinning clusters of young fruits in July.
Centre: Harvesting apples by giving them a gentle twist.
Bottom: Regularly check on stored apples for rot.

Harvesting and storing

The exact time to harvest apples from your trees depends on the variety, growing conditions and where you live. As a general rule, early varieties such as 'Discovery' are ready any time from mid-August onwards, whereas 'Bramley's Seedling' isn't ready to pick until well into October.

To test when the fruit is ready, gently cup it in your hand and give a slight twist. If it's ripe, it will leave the fruiting spur easily without you having to tug! If hard to remove, leave it a few days and try again. When fruits naturally start to drop, that is also an indication that they are ready, and bear in mind that the fruits on the sunny side of the tree will ripen first.

To store apples for later use they need a cool, dark, frost-free place. A shed or garage is ideal as long as it's cool. Early varieties picked in August and September don't tend to store as long as the later fruits that are harvested in October. In the correct conditions, late varieties can often be stored until the following February or March, or even longer.

If possible, store the fruits on trays so that they are not touching and check them on a regular basis. If any start to show signs of rot, remove them straight away.

Powdery mildew – This is a fungal disease that covers the leaves in a powdery white growth, especially the new leaves. It is usually worse in dry soil conditions and when there are heavy dews. Make sure the tree is watered in dry weather and mulch with compost to retain moisture around the roots.

Apple scab – This is another fungal disease that shows as dark scabby areas and cracks on the fruit; the leaves may also discolour and drop prematurely. This is usually more of a problem in wet summers or on trees that are congested. Once peeled, the fruits can still be eaten.

Brown rot – This fungal disease spreads very quickly on many types of fruit while growing on the tree or in storage. The spores enter through a wound and quickly develop. If a healthy fruit touches a diseased fruit, it spreads rapidly. The only way to try and reduce the problem is by removing the fruits and disposing of them as soon as it is spotted. Pruning to an open shape will also help.

Apples in the kitchen

I love to go into our fruit and veg store over the winter months – it's full of onions, potatoes, an odd pumpkin and, of course, apples! As we both come from Nottinghamshire originally, we're big 'Bramley' apple fans and they store really well, getting sweeter with time. 'Newton Wonder' is one of my favourite cookers as well, though, as they keep their shape and taste.

Apple pie with custard or a noggin of cheese has always been a comfort pud in our house all through the winter.

This apple pie recipe is an extra treat with its rich, buttery pastry and hidden surprise. Perfect for Bonfire Night!

Above: Toffee apple pie with a generous serving of custard.
Opposite page: Ellie, our old lab, helping to sort apples for storing.

Toffee apple pie

This amount easily serves 6 to 8 people

Takes about an hour plus an hour chilling time

Ingredients

For the pastry:

I make this pie with a rich, buttery pastry but if time is short then you can buy a ready-made pack of pastry from the supermarket!
120g butter at room temperature
80g caster sugar
Pinch of salt
2 small eggs, beaten
240g plain flour, sieved

For the pie filling:

75g butter
75g granulated sugar
500g cooking apples
175g toffee (I like to use Thornton's toffee – their treacle toffee is perfect for Bonfire Night!)
1 beaten egg for glazing
Caster sugar for sprinkling
Large, deep pie dish

Method

To make the pastry:

› Put the softened butter, sugar and salt together in a bowl and cream together until the mix is pale and fluffy.
› Add the beaten eggs and flour and combine – don't overmix at this stage.
› Cover and pop in the fridge for a good hour.

To make the pie filling:

› Melt the butter and sugar in a large saucepan whilst you core, peel and thickly slice the apples.
› Add the slices to the pan and stir well. Bring to a gentle simmer for 5 minutes. Give a stir occasionally, being careful not to break the apple slices.
› Put into a cold, plastic bowl and pop in the fridge for at least 30 minutes to cool.
› Place the toffee into a strong plastic bag and bash with a rolling pin to break into small chunks.

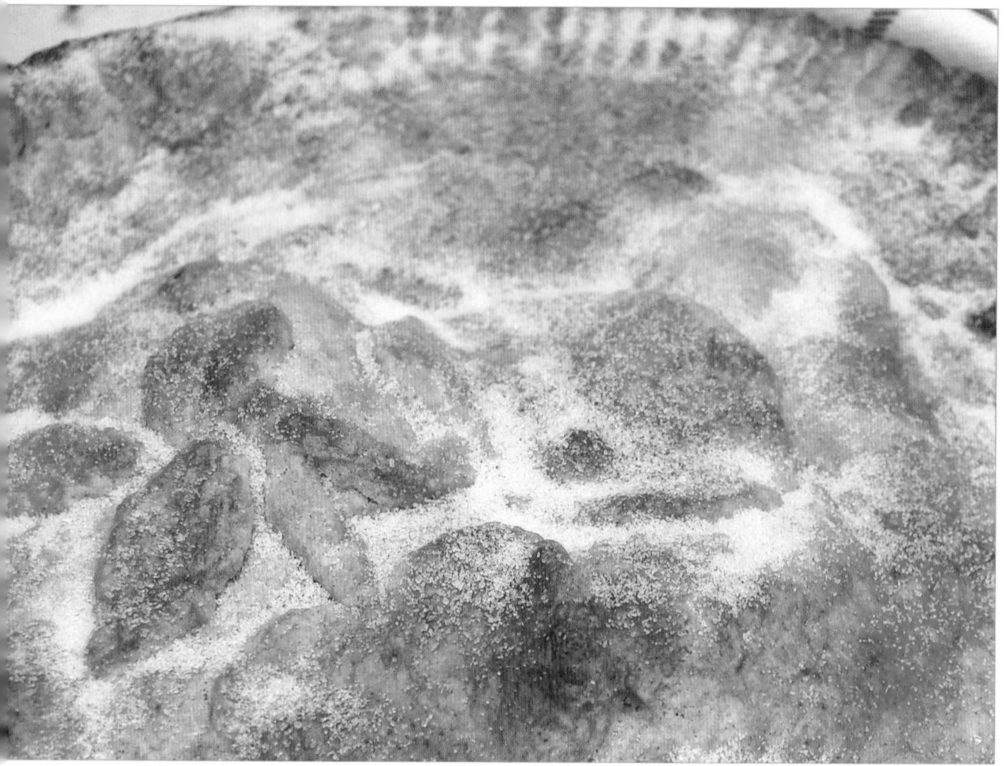

Now for the pie:

- On a well-floured surface, roll out just over half of your pastry to a 5mm thickness and line the dish. Trim off any excess and save the trimmings.
- With the remaining pastry, roll out a lid.
- Lay the cooled apples into the pastry-lined dish and scatter the toffee over the top of the apples.
- Brush the edge of the pastry case with the beaten egg and place the pastry lid on top.
- Press down the edges to seal and trim any excess. Use any trimmings to decorate the top and then glaze the top of the pie with the egg.
- Bake in a preheated oven, 180°C (fan 160°C), gas mark 4, for 30–40 minutes until golden brown.
- As soon as you take the pie from the oven, sprinkle with caster sugar.

We usually have this hot with loads of vanilla ice cream but thick cream or custard is just as good!

Easy no cook – quick sandwich

Try this healthy, fibre and protein-rich lunchtime sandwich - spread some peanut butter on some wholemeal or granary bread then top with thin slices of apple - tasty!

Jill's tips

- If you've only got a few apples to store, put them in a large freezer bag and suck all the air out of it using a straw. Seal tightly then keep in a fridge and they will last for quite a few weeks without any loss of flavour or crispness.
- We grow a variety called 'Red Love' which is a red-fleshed eating apple. It's too tart for me to eat but it magically keeps its colour during cooking so add in to pies and puds for some extra colour. I put some into batches of apple sauce before freezing or bottling to use later in the year – it adds a lovely rosy hue.

Apple flapjack trifle

If you like a trifle, then have a go at this easy recipe - it's something a bit different. I found this in an old apple recipe book that a garden club in East Markham, Nottinghamshire, had made to celebrate their apple day back in 2005! It's easy to make and can be made ahead of time - in fact it improves the flavour of the apples and spices.

Serves 6 generously

Takes about an hour with cooling time

Ingredients

Approx 8 apples - a mix works well or you can use one variety - I like to use 1 cooker in the mix

- 1 tsp cinnamon
- ½ tsp ground nutmeg
- 25g butter
- 25g light muscovado sugar
- 500g carton fresh custard (or make your own)
- 284ml carton double cream, whipped to soft peaks

For the flapjack mix:

- 50g butter
- 100g porridge oats
- 1 tsp mixed spice
- 50g light muscovado sugar

Method

- › To make the flapjack, mix together the oats, spice and sugar. Melt the butter in a small frying pan and tip in the oaty mix. Fry for about 5 minutes until the oats are lightly browned and starting to crisp. Tip into a bowl and leave to cool - they will crisp up more when cool.
- › Peel, core and thickly slice the apples. Melt the 25g batch of butter in a large frying pan until starting to foam and add the apple slices. Fry with a fairly high heat until starting to colour. Turn now and again for about 3 minutes.
- › Add the sugar and spices and cook for another 3 or 4 minutes. The cooking apple (if using) will break down and the eating apples will soften. Check for sweetness and add more sugar if you need it. Leave to cool.

- Layer half the apples and almost half the flapjack mix in your serving bowl then repeat, saving some of the flapjack for the topping.
- Spoon over the custard then carefully top with the cream.

This pud keeps really well for a couple of days in the fridge as it gives the flavours time to develop but it can be eaten straight away too.

When you're ready to serve, scatter over the last of the flapjack mix. If not eating straight away, keep the topping in an airtight tub.

Currants in the garden

As part of the vegetable garden, we have a selection of soft fruit bushes - including blackcurrants and redcurrants that provide a fair amount of fruit in late summer. Soft fruit picked straight from the garden is lovely and much better than shop bought, simply because the delicate fruits don't travel well. It can be cooked, preserved or eaten fresh and we always look forward to picking the crops in late summer. If anyone pops in to visit us while we're picking currants, they're usually roped in to help pick with the reward of a cup of tea and a piece of cake afterwards!

Soil conditions

All soft fruit bushes like a good, fertile soil that is well-drained in winter, but retains moisture in the growing season. Heavy soils can be improved by working in well-rotted manure or garden compost before planting. On lighter soils, the bulky organic matter will help with water and nutrient retention.

Growing methods

I grow our currants as bushes that are pruned to keep them in shape. This method works well as long as you have room to allow the plants to grow properly.

Fortunately, many of the more recent introductions are more compact than some of the old varieties that could grow to be very large.

Redcurrants can also be grown successfully as cordons against a wall or fence. This is basically a single stem that is trained up a cane and as side shoots develop, they are trimmed back in summer to around 5cm (2in). It is on these short

Varieties

Blackcurrant 'Ben Sarek' – Ideal for small gardens or containers as it only grows to around 90cm (36in). It has good disease resistance and produces a heavy crop of large berries.

Blackcurrant 'Ben Connan' – A modern variety that has a compact habit. The fruits are very large and produced in mid-July. It has very good disease resistance and tolerates frost on the flowers.

Blackcurrant 'Big Ben' – As its name implies, it has big, juicy fruits that are ready to harvest in early July. It is also resistant to mildew and leaf spot.

Top: Planting pot grown currants in a new border.
Bottom: Cordon redcurrants against a fence.

stems (spurs) that fruit develops the following year.

Planting

There are two ways of buying currant bushes - containerised and bare-root.

Bare-root bushes are nursery grown and lifted in the autumn when they lose their foliage. Planting of bare-root bushes can be done from November until March. Bushes established in containers are available and can be planted all year round although I prefer to plant in early spring or autumn.

When planting, dig a large hole and fork some well-rotted manure or compost into the base of the hole. Position the plant and backfill with soil, firming as you go.

If planting in winter or spring, I also like to prune the branches hard back after planting to encourage more shoots and a bushy habit.

Aftercare

For the first season after planting, the aim is to encourage a bushy framework of branches. Feed with a general fertiliser when growth starts in spring and keep the area around the plants weed free. For the first summer, water the plants in dry weather.

Once established and fruiting, feed in late winter with sulphate of potash sprinkled around the base of the plants. In mid-spring when the soil is warming up, a light dressing of a general fertiliser can be applied around the roots, followed by a mulch of garden compost. This

Redcurrant 'Laxton's No. 1' – An old variety that produces a crop of redcurrants in July. It does have a spreading habit so needs pruning to maintain its shape.

Redcurrant 'Rovada' – A later-fruiting variety that will carry on cropping into August. The fruits are large and hang in profusion.

Martin's tip

Blackcurrants can be planted a couple of inches lower than they were in the pot so that the base of the stems are buried by a couple of inches of soil. This encourages more shoots to grow from below soil level.

Martin's tip

Don't be tempted to over-feed as it will encourage leaf and stem growth at the expense of fruit.

Top: Shortening new growth on a redcurrant to encourage fat fruiting buds below.
Centre: Old, fruited branch and new branch on a blackcurrant.
Bottom: Starting to prune a redcurrant bush.

will promote healthy growth through the summer months.

Pruning

Blackcurrants grow as a stooled bush with all the growth coming from ground level or below. They fruit on the previous season's growth, meaning the long new shoots produced last summer should flower and fruit this coming year. The aim when pruning is to cut out as much of the old wood as possible, leaving the new stems which are paler and smooth. However, this isn't always possible, because as you cut out the old wood, you also take some of the new shoots with it. To minimise this, always try to prune out branches low down to encourage strong new growth from the base of the plant. Pruning can be done after the fruits have been picked or in winter, or at both times. What you are trying to create is an open bush with a balance of old and new growth to ensure a crop every year.

Pruning for redcurrants is slightly different in the fact that you want to maintain a framework of older branches from which new growth is made. Once a framework of branches has established, in summer cut back the long new growth growing from the older branches to around 5.0cm-7.5cm. It is on the short growths (spurs) that flowers and fruit develop the following year. During the winter you can also thin out some of the older wood if the plant is getting too large and woody. This encourages new replacement growth and keeps the bush healthy. (This pruning method is also used on whitecurrants.)

If growing cordons, they are summer pruned after fruiting by cutting back all the side growth to 5cm (2in).

Harvesting

The exact time to pick your currants will depend on the weather and the variety being grown. However, you will know when it's time to pick simply by tasting the fruits. The longer you leave the currants on the bushes, the sweeter they will become.

Pest and diseases

Gooseberry sawfly – As the name suggests it attacks gooseberries as well as red and white currants. Small caterpillar-like larvae very quickly defoliate the bush, which has a weakening effect. Check for damage from mid-April and pick off the larvae or spray with an insecticide. Nematodes are also available to water over the plants when the larvae are feeding.

Big bud mite – Mainly affects blackcurrants. Microscopic mites enter healthy, pointed buds to feed, causing the buds to swell. There are no treatments available, so pick off large, swollen buds and prune to encourage new growth.

Blackcurrant gall midge – Tiny white maggots feed on new shoots causing stunted growth. Pinching off growing tips with the maggots will help reduce the damage or spray with a suitable insecticide. 'Ben Connan' and 'Ben Sarek' are resistant to the midge.

Above: Netting blackcurrants to keep the birds off.

Opposite, top: Gooseberry sawfly caterpillars.
Centre: Supporting heavy branches on a redcurrant bush.
Bottom: Blackcurrant ' Ben Connan'.

American gooseberry mildew – Affects mainly gooseberries, but occasionally will attack blackcurrants. A white, powdery fungal growth develops on the foliage and fruits, which turn brown with age. There are no fungicides available to control it. Pruning to keep the bush open helps with air circulation. Fortunately, many of the newer varieties are resistant to it.

Currant blister aphid – Affects all currants. Aphids feed on new leaves and cause red swollen blisters to develop. Some insecticides are available for use at certain times of the year. An organic winter wash will help to reduce overwintering eggs.

Birds – Blackbirds and starlings especially love currants and will take them as they ripen. The only sure way to protect the crop is to net them over or grow in a fruit cage.

Bountiful soft fruits from the garden - currants, gooseberries, raspberries and strawberries.

Currants in the kitchen

Currants look like little jewels hanging in the garden. I love watching them ripen and waiting for that perfect moment to catch them at their juicy best. Then it's non-stop – jams and jellies, purée and compotes all get made and stashed away in the store cupboard or freezer waiting to bring a taste of summer to the winter table. Blackcurrants have the most flavour of all the currants – even the leaves smell of the fruits and are a wonderful pick-me-up when crushed!

Redcurrants get made into jelly – I always make loads so that we can use it with gammon, lamb and chicken, and cheeses. It's handy to use as a glaze on fruit tarts too. This year I used half redcurrants with half raspberries for a jelly and it made a fantastic treat to spread on a fresh slice of bread and butter.

Jill's tip

To freeze currants, I line a baking tray with greaseproof paper and lay the fruits on top to go in the freezer. Once frozen, I put them in a freezer bag and suck out all of the air with a straw. When sealed, they should last for a few months without losing any flavour. I often make a mixed bag with raspberries, blackberries and currants ready to add to pies, crumbles and sauces.

Grandma's Yorkshire treat

Martin's become a bit of an expert at Yorkshire puds in our house. I'm afraid I just can't do them – it must be my Nottinghamshire blood! He made a perfect batch last time we had a Sunday roast and it reminded his Mum, Joyce, about a treat her Grandmother used to give them when they were little.

If Grandma Bull had some spare batter mix, she'd throw some red and blackcurrants into it and cook it for the children. With a bit of golden syrup on top, it was a real treat. This is a basic version of a clafoutis – the famous French treat usually made with cherries. I've added a couple of extra ingredients to our Yorkshire pud mix – hope Grandma Bull wouldn't mind!

Serves 2–4

Takes about 30 minutes plus resting time

Ingredients

100g plain flour
2 tblsps caster sugar
2 eggs (weighing 100g), beaten
Dash of vanilla essence
100ml milk (I like to add a dash of double cream as well!)
Butter for greasing
Spoon of caster sugar
2 good handfuls of currants (if frozen, let them thaw first on kitchen paper)
Yorkshire pud tin (about 21cm x 15cm) or muffin tin

Method

› Put the batter ingredients into a large bowl and whisk with a balloon whisk until smooth and frothy. Pour into a jug and pop in the fridge for about half an hour.
› Heat your tin then brush with melted butter and sprinkle over some caster sugar to line the inside.
› Add the currants to the batter then pour into your tin.
› Pop in the oven, 200°C (fan 180°C), gas 6, for about 25 minutes for a large tin or 15 minutes for a muffin tin.

The pud should be crisp and crunchy on the outside and creamy in the middle with bursts of flavour throughout. We always have our Yorkshires with a good squeeze of golden syrup poured over the top but you could add some ice cream if you really wanted too!

Sweet filo horns with summer fruit compote

I inherited lots of my Mum's cooking items for which I'm eternally grateful. They bring back lots of happy memories as Mum was a great cook. A Sunday tea-time treat would sometimes be a cream horn and I have my Mum's cream horn moulds to remind me.

My sister and I would help her wrap flaky pastry round the moulds then when they were crisp and fluffy, we would drop a blob of raspberry jam in the bottom and fill them with whipped cream.

This variation on the classic favourite is quite sweet but the compote can be made as tart as you like.

Serves 4 (2 each)

Takes about 30 minutes plus cooling time

Ingredients

350g frozen currants and berries
Approx 75g caster sugar
Dash of Grand Marnier (optional)
50g unsalted butter, melted, plus a little extra for greasing
4 large sheets filo pastry
125g ricotta cheese
1 tblsp runny honey
15g ground almonds
Handful flaked almonds
Icing sugar to dust
Cream horn moulds

Method

› Tip the fruit and sugar into a saucepan. Heat gently until the fruit is slightly softened and has released lots of juices. Strain, pouring the juices back into the pan. Bring to a simmer then, stirring often, reduce the juices until quite thick.
› Pile the fruit back into the pan and cool, adding Grand Marnier to taste.
› Grease your moulds well and line a baking sheet with greaseproof paper.
› Cut the pastry into 8cm x 16cm squares. Brush with melted butter and fold each one into a triangle.
› Brush the top side of the triangle with butter and wrap around the horn with the pointed end of the triangle to the top. Repeat with the other horns then brush each one all over with butter and lay, seam side down, on the baking tray.
› Pop in the oven, 190°C (fan 170°C), gas 5, for about 10–15 minutes until the

pastry is golden and crispy. Leave to cool on the tray then carefully remove your moulds.

- Heat a frying pan on quite a high heat and add the ground almonds. Toast until just turning brown. Keep an eye on them, though, and keep tossing in the pan. Turn out then repeat with the flaked almonds. Leave to cool.
- Beat together the ricotta cheese, honey and toasted ground almonds.
- Use the end of a spoon or a piping bag to stuff some of the ricotta mixture into each horn, then top with the fruit compote.
- Dust with icing sugar and sprinkle with flaked almonds.

Enjoy for an afternoon tea treat!

Easy no cook – Blackcurrant dressing

Of course, we mustn't forget that currants are great with savoury dishes. Their tartness really cuts through strong flavours like duck, pheasant and venison.

Make a salad dressing with about 2 tablespoons or a thawed ice cube of puree (see Jill's tips right). Mix into a tablespoon of olive oil and ½ tablespoon of balsamic vinegar. Dice a shallot and mix in. Add a dash of water to thin a little. This dressing is perfect on some just-cooled duck on top of some peppery rocket leaves and mixed salad.

Easy cook – Granny Betty's throat soother

I once made some blackcurrant jam that was so well set that you couldn't put a spoon into it - what a disaster! We still used it, though, as my family has a 'secret' recipe that calls for blackcurrant jam no matter how hard it is. It's my Mum's old patent remedy for a bad cough and until now has only ever been given to family!

In a small pan, put a good couple of spoons of jam along with a good squeeze of lemon and a spoon of honey. Melt gently together then pass through a sieve if the jam's got seeds in it. Use this as a thick, soothing drink for a sore throat - I usually dilute it down half and half with boiling water (Martin's been known to add a tot of whisky too!) The purée will keep in the fridge for a few days to use whilst you're suffering!

I'm not sure about the vitamin content of it, but it always worked when we were little and it's a favourite of our son Richard, when he gets a bout of tonsillitis!

Jill's tips

Make a purée which you can freeze to use later in the year with sweet or savoury dishes. Put 300g mixed currants in a pan with about 35ml water. Heat to a gentle simmer then cook for 5–10 minutes until the currants are really soft. Push through a sieve, removing the skins and seeds, and scatter in about 50g of icing sugar.

I always freeze this in individual portions (use an ice cube tray) so that I can mix one into yoghurt for a quick pud.

Alternatively, add to a glass of milk in a blender for a blackcurrant smoothie – you could add a handful of oats to make a delicious breakfast drink.

Pears in the garden

Homegrown pears are delicious and can be eaten at exactly the stage of ripeness that you enjoy. I prefer a firm pear (so to speak!) but Jill likes them when they are fully ripe and very juicy. Pears need more warmth and sunshine than apples, which is perhaps the reason they are not as popular in gardens. Given the correct growing conditions they grow well and you can get some heavy crops. Some varieties also like more warmth than others so I'm afraid the further north you live the smaller the choice is. Wherever you live, a warm, sheltered spot is essential to protect the early blossom. We grow '**Conference**' in our small orchard and it produces a good crop most years.

Soil conditions

Good soil conditions are essential for healthy growth. Pears need a moisture retaining soil, but they will not stand waterlogged conditions in the winter. A free-draining loamy soil is ideal with plenty of organic matter. Avoid shallow chalky or wet, acid soils as the trees will struggle.

The position is also very important and you should plant the trees where they get maximum sunlight and protection from cold, northerly winds. Against a south facing wall is ideal or where the trees are protected by other trees.

Pear root stocks

Quince rootstocks are commonly used when budding and grafting pears. 'Quince A' is the most vigorous of the two and produces trees of up to 5.5m (18ft) and 'Quince C' is slightly smaller at 4m (13ft). Not sure what happened to 'Quince B'! Both A & C make good garden trees that don't grow too large.

Varieties

We grow '**Conference**' and '**Williams**' in our garden and I've listed others that are all suitable for growing in the north. They will of course grow very well in the south where it's a little warmer. Pears need a pollinator, which is basically another variety of pear in flower at the same time, so plant two or more if you have room. A self-fertile pear will fruit on its own, although it will produce a better crop if there is a nearby pollinator.

'**Conference**' – probably the most popular home-grown pear because it is self-fertile and reliable. It produces long, narrow fruits that will keep for up to 2 months after picking.

An old, trained espalier pear tree.

Planting

Planting of bare-root trees is done from late November until late February while they are dormant. Prepare the soil before planting by deep digging to loosen any hard layers and if the soil needs improving work in some organic matter to the area in advance. Dig a large hole, position the tree in the hole and knock in the tree stake. Back fill and firm the soil as you go, making sure the existing soil mark is at soil level and the graft above soil level. Finally, secure the trunk to the stake with a rubber tie and leave the stake in position for a couple of years until the roots have established.

Trees grown in pots can be planted all year round as there is no root disturbance, but I prefer to do it either in spring or autumn if possible when the soil is moist. Before planting, water the roots and water again after planting.

Tree shapes

Just like apples, pears can be trained in a number of different shapes which allows you to be able to grow them in gardens large and small.

The most common shapes are half-standards, bush, cordon, espalier and fan, but they are very versatile and can be trained into just about any shape you want, including arches and pyramids.

Trained fruit trees such as cordons and espaliers for growing against a wall or fence can be bought partially trained or you can train your own.

Most pears are sold as multi-stemmed trees that can easily be trained into a bush shape on a short trunk to create a manageable sized tree.

'**Invincible**' – a recent introduction that is ideal for growing in the north because it flowers over a long period and is self-fertile. The fruits are sweet and juicy and can be picked over several weeks and will store for a few months.

'**Beurre Hardy**' – an old French pear with a lovely flavour that is also suitable for cooler conditions. It produces large, sweet pears that should be picked under-ripe and allowed to ripen in store.

'**Williams' Bon Chretien**' – an old English dessert pear often known as '**Williams**' or '**Bartletts**' (it's often tinned). It has a wonderful flavour when ripe and will grow in the north in a sheltered spot.

'**Beth**' – a lovely pear that is suitable for the north and produces a fruit with a good, sweet flavour. It flowers over a long period making it a good pollinator.

'**Black Worcester**' – a very old English cooking pair that has been grown since the 16th century. It produces medium sized, hard, dark fruits that are picked late and used in cooking and preserves.

Top: Pear blossom.
Centre: Fruits of '**Black Worcester'** pear.
Bottom: Thinning pears in early summer to reduce the crop.

Pruning

The pruning of pears is the same as apples. Most pears grow very well as spur bearers, which also helps to keep the tree compact. If training a bush tree, in winter prune out the central main lead stem back to a side branch and prune back the other side branches by half to encourage bushy growth. The aim is to create a 'wine glass' shape as you would when pruning an apple.

The natural habit of pears tends to be upright, so if the tree develops several straight vertical branches these can be trimmed back to an outward facing bud. The following winter the new growth is also pruned back by around half and by that point the basic framework of branches should be starting to develop.

Once there is a good shaped framework you can if you wish start some summer pruning to develop a spur system. This is done in late summer around August and all you do is simply cut back the new season's growth to a couple of buds. It's on these short growths (spurs) that flower buds develop for the following year. Once you start this system of summer pruning it needs to be done every summer to maintain the shape and size of the tree.

If you want the tree to be a little larger, or want a new branch to grow and fill a space, simply leave some of the summer growth un-pruned for a year or two.

Pears can also be pruned hard back if you need to. This might be because they have grown too tall or wide. Hard pruning should be done in winter and the following August you can thin and re-shape the tree.

Trained cordons and espaliers are also pruned annually in August in the same way. Cutting back the new growth to a couple of buds maintains the shape and it allows more sunshine to the developing fruits.

Martin's tip

Feeding around the base of fruit trees in late winter/early spring with a few handfuls of sulphate of potash will help flower formation and the development of fruit in the summer.

Harvesting and storing

The basic test to see if a pear is ready is to hold the fruit gently and give a twist. If it leaves the tree easily, it's ready to pick and eat straight from the tree. However, some are best picked from the tree before they are ripe and then allowed to ripen in store. My favourite, '**Conference**', can be picked and eaten fresh while the flesh is hard and crisp, which is exactly how I like them. They can also be stored in cool conditions and over several weeks they will soften and become juicy and sweeter, which is how Jill likes them. Other varieties such as '**Beurre Hardy**' and '**Comice**' are usually picked slightly under-ripe and allowed to ripen in store.

Martin's tip

If you are unsure when the pears are ready to harvest, pick one and try it! If it's too hard try again in a few days.

Pest and diseases

Pears tend to suffer from the same problems as apples, such as codling moth and scab (see 'Apples'). There are, however, also some problems that are specific to pears.

Pear blister mite - A microscopic mite that enters the new leaves in spring to feed on sap. They cause pale blisters to develop in the leaves, which by late summer will turn black. There are no treatments available to control the mites. If only a few leaves are affected, pick them off and burn, but if the whole tree is attacked, removing all the leaves is more harmful to the tree than the mites. Well established trees will still fruit, despite the infestation.

Pear midge - This is a serious pest that can ruin a crop. The small midges lay their eggs in the pear blossom and the small larvae feed inside the fruitlets. The first sign is often when the small pears turn black and fall to the ground in June. When split open, you will find tiny grubs. Some insecticides can be

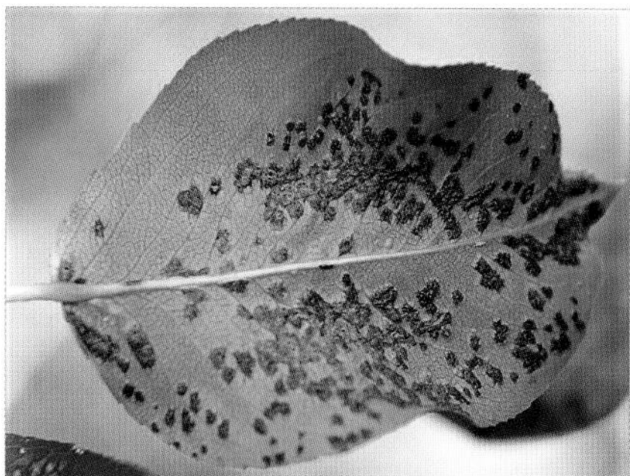

Top: Pear blister mite.
Bottom: Pear rust.

sprayed just before the blossom opens to control the larvae. Alternatively, pick all the fallen fruits to prevent the larvae pupating in the soil below the tree.

Pear rust - This is a fungal disease that attacks the foliage and is very easy to recognise by the bright-orange spots on the upper surface of the leaves, followed by warty growths underneath. There are no treatments available to control rust on pears. Although tempting to pick off the damaged leaves, the green part still produces food for the plant so the foliage should be left on. In autumn, clear away fallen leaves to reduce re-infection. Juniper is also a host of pear rust and is often the source of infection.

Blossom wilt - This fungal disease can affect all fruit trees. The blossoms wither after opening and remain dead on the tree. No treatments are available and dead blossom should be trimmed off to prevent it spreading to the foliage.

A slice of Pear and ginger pavlova.

Pears in the kitchen

We used to have an old, gnarled '**Conference**' pear tree at the bottom of our garden that I used to climb when we were little, but nobody ever told me not to eat the pears straight from the tree unless they were perfectly ripe and I remember them being like bullets whenever I picked one. I still get a bit impatient waiting for pears to ripen and I can still never quite tell when that perfect moment is!

The '**Conference**' tree in our orchard does really well and last year I counted 168 pears! The pears store well, fortunately, which gives me time to make lots of delicious treats. I usually make a chutney with orange and ginger, lots of puree and I always end up bottling the last batch.

Easy cook – pear and apple compote

I put about 6 peeled and chopped pears into my slow cooker along with a mix of about 6 peeled and chopped cooking and eating apples. I then add in a couple of tablespoons of brown sugar and water and a good handful of dried fruit (cranberries are perfect). This is great done overnight then in the morning you come down to a fabulous smell and it's cooked down to a tasty compote. We eat it with some yoghurt or Martin will have it on top of his breakfast porridge. A tubful will keep well in the fridge for quite a few days so we can dip into it whenever we want.

Jill's tips

- It's worth puréeing some pears to freeze and eat later. It's easy to do – just peel, core and cube the pears, then simmer until tender in either just water or a sweetened water, depending on what they will be used for. Drain, then blitz in a liquidiser, then freeze in small portions, ready to use – you could add it to some rice pud or custard for a comfort pud or use in a fool or with ice cream. Try adding some purée to mashed parsnips – trust me, it works, especially with a pork chop.
- Have some acidulated water on standby to keep your pears pale. Simply squeeze half a lemon into a bowl of water and drop pears into it whilst you're prepping them for cooking.

Pear and ginger pavlova

I inherited my love of Pavlova from my mum as she used to make it for everyone's birthday treat. In those days it was always topped with After Eight mints cut into triangles and she would push some chopped up mints into the squidgy mallow middle! Now I often make one for groups visiting our garden at lunchtime and there's never any leftover as it still seems to be everyone's favourite, especially when topped with cream and fresh berries.

For a more autumnal treat I've topped this one with pears and ginger to add a warming spiciness to our favourite pud.

Serves 8 generously. Takes about 2 hours plus cooling time but can be made ahead the day before ready to assemble

For the pavlova:

4 large egg whites
225g caster sugar
1tsp vanilla essence
1tsp white vinegar

For the topping:

6 ripe pears
Good squeeze lemon juice
50g caster sugar
Water
7 or 8 bulbs of stem ginger, chopped finely
300ml double cream

Method - for the pavlova:

› Cut out a rectangle of greaseproof paper to fit a baking tray and put it on the upturned side of the tray (this makes it easier to slide the pavlova off when it's cooled without cracking it).
› Whisk the egg whites with an electric whisk until they are stiff and form peaks. Add a tablespoon of sugar and whisk in thoroughly then repeat until all the sugar has been added. Keep the whisk on maximum all the time, it's important that the sugar is mixed in well otherwise your pavlova will weep a sticky syrup after cooking.
› Slow the whisk down to medium and add the vinegar and vanilla essence and mix in.
› Use a palette knife to spread the pavlova mix onto your baking sheet in a

Gardening on the Menu
Pear & chocolate
jam

rectangle so that it's about 5cm high and 28cmx18cm. Smooth round the sides and top - it doesn't have to be a perfect finish! Of course you could make a more traditional circle but I find a rectangle easier to cut into portions.

- Pop into the oven at 140°C (fan120), gas 1, and bake for an hour and a quarter then turn the oven off and leave the pavlova to cool in the oven.
- The pavlova will keep well for at least a couple of days in an airtight tub, leave it on the greaseproof paper - it's easier to move around without breaking.

For the pear topping:

- Put the lemon juice and about 150ml of water in a saucepan.
- Peel the pears with a potato peeler then quarter, remove the cores and chop into bite size pieces. Put the pieces straight into the saucepan. Add the sugar and enough water to only just cover the pears.
- Simmer over a low heat for 5-10 minutes, depending on the ripeness of your pears. Leave in the syrup to cool. This keeps well in the fridge until needed.

To finish the pavlova:

- Drain a good half of the pears and whip the cream to soft peaks.
- Stir the chopped ginger and the drained pears gently into the cream.
- Carefully take the lining paper from the pavlova and place on a serving plate.
- Spoon on the cream and spread out over the pavlova. Ruffle up with a fork and dot an extra few pieces of pear over the top.

Serve this at room temperature with some of the spare pears in syrup on the side.

Pear and chocolate jam

My favourite pear recipe has to be this pear and chocolate jam - it's not a healthy option but I say 'a little of what you fancy!'

Makes about 6 medium size jars and takes about an hour (most of which is peeling and chopping!).

1kg just ripe pears
Juice of 2 large lemons
Tbsp of water
800g granulated sugar
Good pinch of cinnamon
150g dark chocolate (min 70% cocoa solids)
Sterilised jars and lids
Plate in the freezer to test for set

- Chop the chocolate and put to one side ready to use.
- Use a potato peeler to peel the pears then quarter them and take out the cores. Dice into fairly small chunks.
- Tip into your preserving pan with a tablespoon of water and the lemon juice.
- Heat gently then cook slowly for just 5 minutes, stirring often.
- Turn the heat right down and add the sugar and the cinnamon. Stir until the sugar has dissolved then bring up to a boil and cook for 10-15 minutes.
- Turn the heat off and test for set using your frozen saucer- put a teaspoon of jam on the saucer and leave for a minute. Push your finger through the jam. If it wrinkles - it's ready.
- You're looking for a soft set - if it's not ready turn up the heat and test after another 2 or 3 minutes.
- Keep the heat low and stirring constantly add the chocolate. Stir until it's thoroughly melted.
- Pot up into warm jars and seal.

This is scrumptious as an ice cream topping or to have with brioche or croissant for breakfast. Or as a topping for pancakes or waffles. Yum yum yum!!

Quick recipes - savoury pears

Don't forget that pears work well in a lot of savoury dishes too:

- To really bring out the flavour of the pears try griddling them first. Heat a griddle pan (or your grill) and cook sliced pears for a few minutes on each side until browned and just softened.
- Gently toss some slices of warm griddled pear in some honey and mustard dressing. Pile onto some wholemeal bread and crumble over some blue cheese and add a scattering of chopped walnuts - delicious!
- Make a salad with some fresh salad leaves topped with thinly sliced pears. Add some sliced soft brie and a dressing made from 3 parts oil, 1 part raspberry vinegar. Toss gently together and finish with a few crushed raspberries.

Jill's tip

Try roasting pears – leave the peel on but halve fruits and scoop out the core with a spoon. Drizzle over a little honey and scatter on some cinnamon or ginger and roast for about 20 minutes (oven 190C (fan 170), gas 5). If you like you could crush a ginger biscuit and scatter over the pear half way through the cooking time. Serve with some creamy vanilla ice cream.

Easy cook - bottled pears

Peel, halve or quarter and core your pears then simmer for about 5 minutes till only just tender in a sugar syrup (about 200g of sugar to 1 litre of water) with maybe some cinnamon or a vanilla pod and some orange zest. Put the pears and some fresh orange zest into sterilised jars, cover with syrup and add a little glug of brandy to the jar before sealing. Perfect for the winter or to give as presents at Christmas. If you want a long shelf life then submerge sealed jars in boiling water for about 20 minutes.

Quick cook – Sticky cinnamon pears

Dissolve 150g brown sugar in 500ml of water and add a good pinch of ground cinnamon. Add some peeled, cored and quartered pears and simmer for about 15 minutes until tender. Remove the pears then boil up the syrup for about 5 minutes until it's thick and sticky and serve poured over the pears.

Raspberries in the garden

Raspberries are one fruit that we would grow wherever we lived. The ripe berries are delicious and just melt in your mouth to release that sweet, tangy flavour. Without a doubt one of the great things about growing your own raspberries is the freshness of the ripe fruit and that wonderful, just-picked flavour. It's always a pleasure to pick them and as part of the process you just have to taste them – it's one for the bowl and one for me!

Growing raspberries is not difficult and once the plants, known as canes, are established in the garden they will grow and fruit for many years with just a small amount of attention at various times of the year.

There are two groups of raspberries and both are very simple to grow as long as you follow the basic pruning rules, which we'll look at later.

Summer raspberries fruit from early July until around the middle of August and they produce their berries on the previous season's canes. Autumn raspberries fruit on current season's growth and start to crop from mid to late August through until October or the first frost of the autumn. Both types are very productive and if you are able to have some of each type in your garden it means you can enjoy fresh raspberries for around four months. At Thornycroft we grow both types for that very reason and they are all put to good use in the kitchen.

Soil conditions

To grow well, raspberries need a fertile, well-drained, moisture-retentive soil. Heavy clay soils can be improved by working in plenty of garden compost or well-rotted manure which will open up the soil and improve drainage. Light, sandy soils that dry out quickly also benefit from the addition of compost or manure as this acts like a sponge, helping the soil to hold on to moisture in dry weather. The addition of this bulky organic matter also helps to make the soil

Varieties

There are many different varieties to choose from, and all are delicious. For summer raspberries I'm growing **'Glen Ample'** which does very well and is a strong grower. The autumn raspberries in our garden are **'Joan J'**. I've been growing this variety for over 10 years and it never fails to produce a heavy crop.

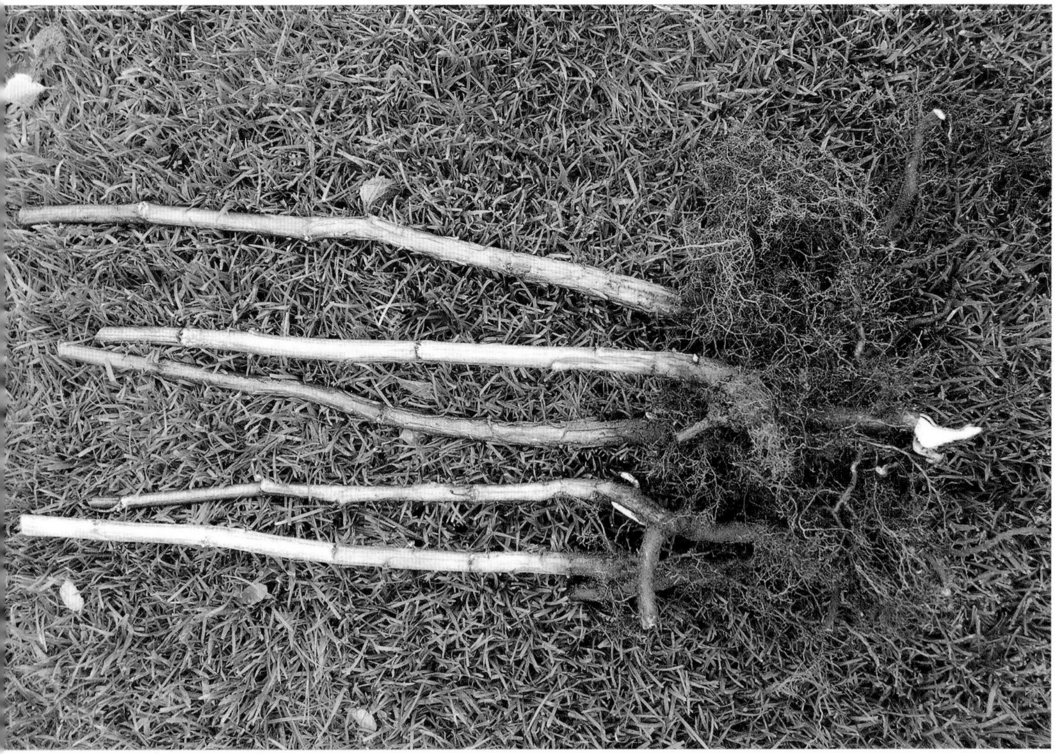

Top: Bare rooted canes ready to plant.
Left: Summer raspberry canes tied to wires.

slightly acidic which is just what raspberries like. They also prefer a good light position where they get sun for most of the day, although they will tolerate some dappled shade for part of the day.

Planting

Most raspberries tend to be sold as bare-root canes for planting in the dormant season between November and February. The ground should have been prepared in advance by digging it over to remove any weeds and to mix in the organic matter.

Plant the canes approximately 40cm (16in) apart in a single row. If you want to plant more than one row, allow around 1.5m (5ft) between rows. Plant the canes so that the roots are just below the surface of the soil, or if you can see the original soil mark on the base of the cane, use that as a guide. Once you've planted, make sure the roots are well firmed in to prevent them from blowing around in the soil.

When you buy raspberry canes they are usually partly cut down for ease of handling and planting. Once planted, the canes should be cut down lower to around 30cm (12in) from ground level. In early spring, give the plants their final prune by cutting them down to ground level - literally level with the soil. This encourages new shoots to grow from dormant buds just below ground level. The planting and initial pruning is the same for both summer and autumn fruiting raspberries.

It is also possible to buy raspberry canes growing in pots for summer planting, but these

Summer fruiting

'Malling Minerva' – An early variety with very good disease resistance. The canes are spineless and the red fruits are produced from mid-June for around six weeks.

'Malling Jewel' – A late summer variety with large, dark red fruits. The canes are strong growing and have a good resistance to root rots.

'Glen Ample' – A heavy cropping mid-season variety with good disease resistance. The plants produce vigorous, spineless upright canes and the large red fruits are borne from July into August.

'Octavia' – A late season variety that fills the gap between the last of the summer varieties and the first of the autumn types. Large red fruits are produced until mid-August.

'Ruby Beauty' – A dwarf raspberry that only grows to 'm (3ft) tall that is ideal for growing in large pots on a patio. It's thornless and starts producing red berries from mid-summer.

Martin's tip

In dry weather I water along the row to keep the plants healthy and growing. This is particularly important when the berries are starting to develop and swell. To seal in the moisture around the roots I mulch along the row with fresh grass clippings.

Autumn fruiting

'All Gold' – A yellow fruiting variety that produces masses of very sweet berries from mid-August until the first frosts.

'Joan J' – A spineless autumn raspberry that produces a very high yield of large red berries well into October.

Top: Pruning autumn raspberries to ground level in early spring.
Left: Pruning out old fruited canes on summer raspberries, leaving the young canes for next year.

will be more expensive and I find they don't establish as well as bare-root canes planted in the winter. Where possible I always prefer to get the canes planted and established in the dormant season.

Supporting raspberries

Most varieties of raspberry will grow to between 1.5m and 2.1m (5ft and 7ft) tall and will need to be supported to keep them upright. The traditional method is to have a series of horizontal wires strung between posts to which the canes can be tied with string. This single post system is mainly used on summer raspberries where the old canes are cut out in late summer and the new ones tied in.

Alternatively, double rows of posts and wires can be used spaced 60cm (2ft) apart. The raspberries are planted in the middle of the rows and as they grow the two sets of wires give them support and keep them upright. This is a really simple method and tends to work better on the autumn varieties that are completely cut down each year.

Growing raspberries in a small area

Where space in the garden is limited, raspberries can be grown up a single post. Simply plant two or three canes at the base of a wooden post and as the canes grow, loop string around them and the post for support.

Another method is to create a wigwam out of bamboo garden canes and as the raspberries grow they can be tied to the bamboo canes to create a compact fruiting wigwam.

Container growing

It's also possible to grow raspberries in large pots of compost, preferably with some loam-based compost added. In a pot they will grow and fruit for several years as long as you keep the plants well watered and fed with a liquid fertiliser through the growing season. I've tried growing in pots and find autumn types that are pruned down completely in March work best.

Pruning and feeding

This is the bit where people often get confused, but pruning is very simple as long as you know what type of raspberries you are growing - summer or autumn.

Summer raspberries are pruned in late summer when fruiting finishes. All the old fruited canes are cut out to ground level to make way for the new developing canes that will carry next year's crop. Distinguishing between the old and new canes is simple as the older ones that have fruited are brown and have the remains of the old flower stalks, whereas the young canes will be fresh and green. It's simply a case of out with the old and in with the new.

Autumn fruiting varieties are pruned in late winter/early spring by cutting all the canes down to ground level. In my garden, I like to do it towards the end of February or early March, depending on the weather. This hard pruning encourages strong new canes to grow from dormant buds below ground level and by mid-summer these canes will be around 1.2m–1.5m (4ft–5ft) tall and starting to produce flowers at the tips of the shoots.

All raspberries will benefit from a general feed in spring just as new growth emerges. A general fertiliser, such as Growmore, blood, fish and bone or dried poultry pellets, is ideal as it supplies a good range of nutrients needed for healthy growth. A mulch of garden compost spread along the rows will help to retain moisture in the soil and, of course, it helps to prevent weeds from growing.

Harvesting

We always look forward to the first raspberries of the season and you'll know when they are ripe because you'll be testing them on a regular basis! When ripe, the berries should be easy to pull off the stalk. If you have to pull hard, they are not ripe and can be left a few more days. Ideally, pick on a regular basis to encourage more to ripen.

Pest and diseases

Raspberries, like many other fruits, can suffer from their fair share of pests and diseases. However, when they are grown well, in good soil, and are pruned properly, the chances of many diseases are reduced.

Raspberry beetle - The main pest on raspberries is caused by the raspberry beetle which lays her eggs on the developing fruits. These hatch out into small white maggots that can be found when the fruit is harvested. Traps that hang in the row can be used to lure the female moths into them; these work well and vastly reduce the damage to the berries.

Birds - Birds can also be a problem as they love the ripe berries. I find it is mainly the summer varieties that are attacked and to protect them they need to be covered over with nets. We don't protect our autumn raspberries from the birds as they don't seem to bother them. Perhaps they've had their fill by September!

Raspberry chocolate pot.

Raspberries in the kitchen

If I could only grow one fruit in a garden then it would have to be raspberries. Raspberries, cream and a crushed meringue make a perfect pud for me and when they're picked fresh from the canes they taste magnificent. Often I've eaten most of the bowlful by the time I get to the kitchen! Molly our mad cocker spaniel is quite partial to them as well and she'll graze the lower fruits and catch any that miss my bowl!

There's so much that you can do with them - add to smoothies and juices, pop inside a Victoria sandwich, ginger snaps or rich chocolate brownies or make jams and ice cream. The perfect ingredient.

Easy no-cook recipe - Raspberry brandy snaps

Buy some brandy snap baskets and fill them with a lemony cream made from whipped double cream and a good dollop of lemon curd. Top with fresh raspberries and maybe a drizzle of raspberry puree. Yum!

Jill's tips

I always make a raspberry puree if there's a glut by simply sieving the fruits with some icing sugar to remove the seeds. It freezes perfectly so I can use it as a sauce for loads of puds over the year – a real taste of summer.

Peach Melba jam

This raspberry recipe is one I've passed on to loads of people and I've never known anyone to say it hasn't worked! The flavour is strongly of raspberries but the peaches give it an extra sweetness hit. A classic combination.

Don't spend a fortune on peaches - supermarkets often have them in the 'reduced' section as they are brought in far too early and quickly reach their 'sell by' date. They are perfect for this recipe when mixed with your home grown raspberries so keep your eye out for a bargain when your raspberries are ready.

Makes 3-4 x 454g (1lb) jars

Preparation: 20 minutes

Cooking: 15-20 minutes plus overnight soaking and cooling

Ingredients

500g raspberries
500g peaches, halved and stoned, then diced quite small
800g jam sugar
juice 1 lemon
Sterilised jam jars and lids or seals (see the cooks' notes in the Introduction)

Method

- The night before you make your jam, layer the berries, peaches and sugar in a large bowl. Cover and set aside at room temperature.
- The next morning it will look as if it's starting to ferment as the fruit will have released loads of juice and the sugar will be bubbling up a bit. Give everything a good stir and set aside again until you're ready to start cooking.

This is such a quick cook jam that you need to get everything ready before you start to cook so:

- Put a small saucer in the freezer ready to test for jam set.
- Sterilise your jars and lids in readiness
- Now get everything else ready - I tend to get teaspoons, paper towels and pouring jugs ready along with trivets for the hot pan and trays of jars.

Finally the jam!

- Tip the raspberries and peaches, scraping out all the juices and any undissolved sugar, into a preserving pan (or use a large, wide-based pan - the wider and more open the pan, the faster the jam will be ready without the fruit cooking to mush).
- Stir in the lemon juice and cook over a very low heat until any remaining sugar has dissolved.
- Bring the mixture to the boil, then simmer for 5 minutes stirring now and again.
- Turn off the heat and spoon a little of the hot jam onto the chilled saucer. Leave for a minute then push the jam with your finger - if it wrinkles a little, it has reached setting point. If it's still too runny to wrinkle, return the pan to the heat and boil in 2-min stages, removing the pan from the heat each time you repeat the saucer test, until ready.
- Skim off any scum with a spoon and give another stir.
- Remove your jars from the oven and use a small jug to pour in the jam. Wipe any

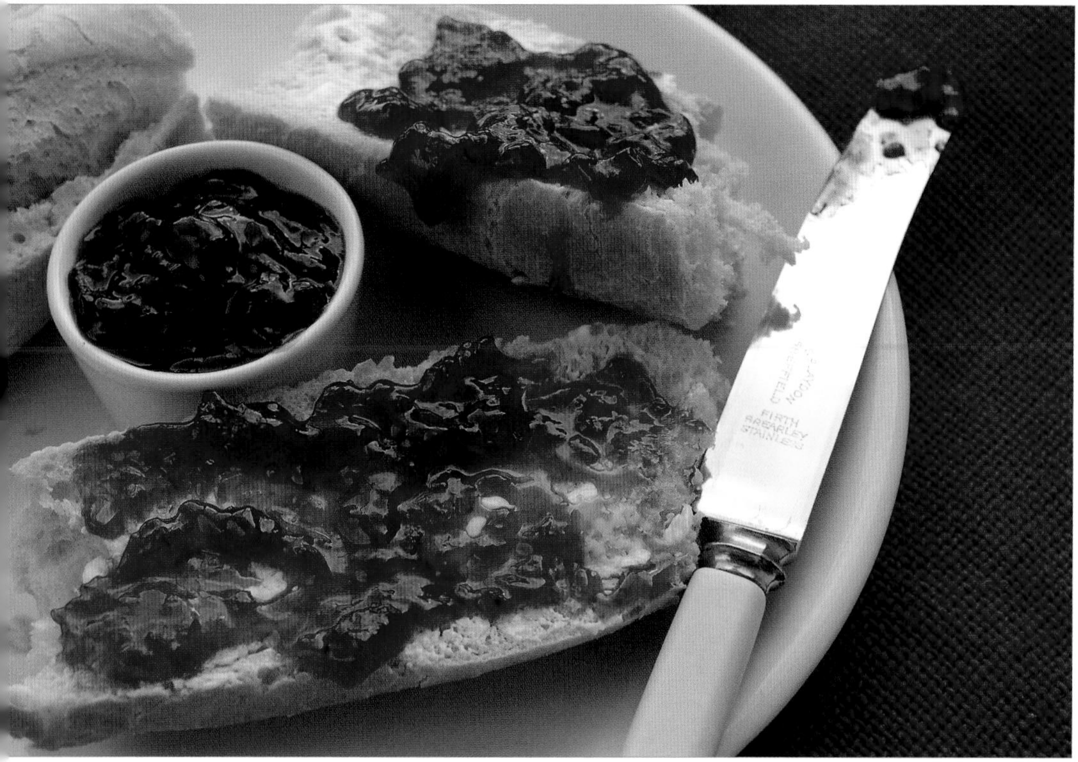
FIRTH
BREARLEY
STAINLESS

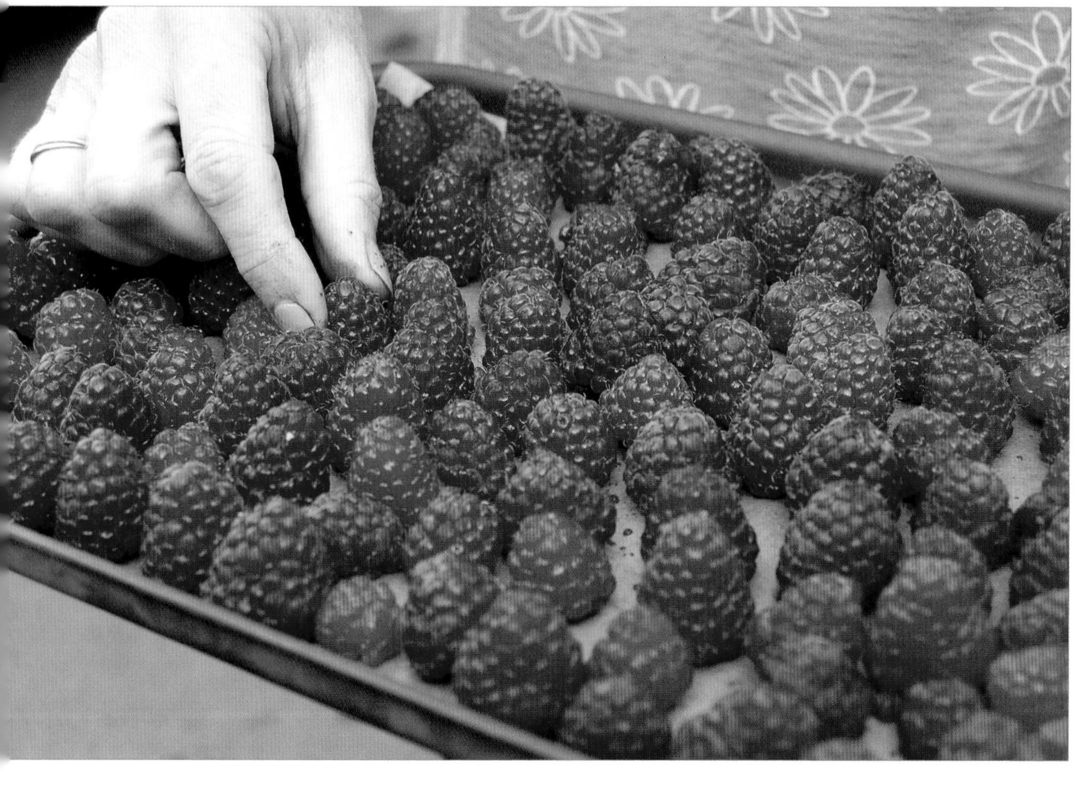

spills as you go. Fill right to the top and seal immediately with the lids, screwing them on tightly. Alternately pop on a waxed circle then leave to cool and seal with a cellophane top.

Leave to cool then label and store in a cool dark cupboard. This jam should keep for 6 months to a year without losing any flavour - if you don't eat it by then! Once it's opened though you should keep it in the fridge.

Enjoy with fresh crusty bread - personally I like a fresh, crusty baguette!

Easy no cook recipe - Raspberry chocolate pots

Try this for a scrummy pud with chocolate and raspberries - what's not to love! See p262 for picture.

Melt a mix of dark and milk chocolate and leave to cool then add in double the amount of Greek yoghurt and a drizzle of honey to taste.

Lightly crush some raspberries and put in a serving dish then pile on the chocolate topping.

Grate over some chocolate to enjoy!

Jill's tips

- When you get a glut raspberries freeze really well. Line a baking tray with greaseproof paper or a silicone sheet and spread out the raspberries in a single layer. Pop in the top of the freezer until solid then lift off and seal in a freezer bag, sucking the air out with a straw. Because they've frozen separately you can use them as you need them rather than having a frozen block of raspberries.
- If you're making a Bakewell tart using raspberry jam, pop some fresh raspberries onto the jam layer before adding the frangipane topping. They taste delicious!

Opposite:
Bottom: Open freeze raspberries before packing in bags.

Rhubarb in the garden

As a child, I seem to remember everyone growing a clump of rhubarb in their garden and I used to wander up to my Grandma's garden to pull a few sticks of rhubarb which I would then dip into a small bowl of sugar! It was always sour, but with plenty of sugar it was fine. I still love rhubarb and look forward to the first tender sticks in spring.

Although technically a vegetable, we all tend to think of rhubarb as a fruit and, of course, it is mostly eaten as a pudding. It's a hardy perennial that is reasonably easy to grow and once established in the garden, it will thrive for many years as long as you give it some basic maintenance each year. For it to grow well, it does need a period of cold weather in winter to break its dormancy and start it back into growth in spring.

Soil conditions

Rhubarb will grow in most soil conditions, but ideally it prefers a fertile, moisture-retentive, well-drained soil and plenty of sun. Although it likes moisture when growing, it certainly doesn't like waterlogged soil in the winter as this can lead to the roots rotting. It is quite greedy, so when preparing the soil for planting, work in plenty of well-rotted farmyard manure or garden compost to improve the soil. It will tolerate a little dappled shade for part of the day but, if possible, position the plant where it will get maximum light.

Planting

Most rhubarb is planted as root divisions known as crowns from mid-autumn through until early spring when the root is dormant. It can be grown from seed, but it takes a couple of years

Varieties

Many people have clumps of rhubarb given to them by friends and don't know which variety it is, but if you are buying new crowns, there are several named varieties to choose from. We have three crowns in our garden, but I'm not sure what they are, although I suspect one is **'Victoria'**.

'Timperley Early' – An early variety that can also be forced. It produces long, thin stems with a good flavour.

'Early Champagne' – Another naturally early type that has a sweet flavour.

Top: Divide a large root of rhubarb to make two new plants.
Bottom: New shoots emerging in early spring.

before you get any stalks to pull and it doesn't always come true from seed. I think it's better to buy a named variety or get a division from a friend's established clump.

Plant the root in well-prepared soil so that the large buds on top of the crown are more or less at soil level and firm the soil around the root. If you are planting more than one crown, space them around 90cm (3ft) apart.

'Cawood Delight' – A good, reliable variety that has dark-red stalks.

'Victoria' – A later variety that can be pulled into August. A strong grower with good flavour.

Aftercare

With newly planted rhubarb, you shouldn't pull any sticks in the first year as it really weakens the plant while it is establishing. Through the first growing season, water in dry weather and feed around the roots with a general fertiliser to encourage plenty of stalks and large leaves.

In autumn when the weather starts to cool down, the foliage will turn yellow and the fleshy stalks will collapse. All the old plant can be removed and added to the compost heap to expose the top of the crown to the winter elements. A mulch of compost or manure can be applied in late winter or early spring, but do not completely cover the crown, instead spread the mulch around the crown in a circle like a doughnut.

In spring, the buds will start into growth and at this point a couple of handfuls of fertiliser can be sprinkled around the plant to give it a good supply of nutrients.

In late spring and early summer, it's not unusual for rhubarb to flower. The thick flower buds are obvious and as soon as they develop, the thick stems should be cut off so that the plant can divert its energy into making more stalks.

Martin's tip

Rhubarb leaves contain oxalic acid and are poisonous, but they can be added to the compost heap where they rot down very quickly.

Top: Covering an established clump with a traditional forcing pot.
Bottom: Forced rhubarb in mid-March.

Dividing old clumps

The rhubarb roots will get bigger each year and produce more stalks, but after several years the plant will start to get tired and the centre of the large clump will die out. To keep a clump healthy and vigorous, it pays to lift and divide the clump every four or five years. This is done in the dormant season and is simply a case of digging out the large root and using a spade, chop it into several smaller pieces, making sure each one has at least one fat bud, but preferably two or three. The old, woody centre of the root can be thrown away.

Forcing

For an early crop of pink rhubarb, you can force a clump into growth. It's very simple and all you do is cover over an established clump in late winter, around February, with a container which can be a terracotta forcing pot, an upturned dustbin or a large pot. To help speed up the forcing you can cover the crown over with some dry leaves or straw to help raise the temperature slightly and then spread some fresh manure around the outside of the pot, again to create heat and start the rhubarb into growth. This isn't necessary, but it does encourage very early growth. After a few weeks, check inside the pot and after a month or two you should be able to pull forced rhubarb.

Once you have harvested the forced sticks, remove the cover and allow the clump to carry on growing through the summer without any more sticks being pulled. This lets the crown build up its strength again. If you intend to force every spring, ideally you need two or three clumps so that they can be forced in rotation. This way the clumps are not exhausted and remain healthy and vigorous.

Harvesting

Start to harvest the sticks of rhubarb from un-forced clumps from April onwards. The exact timing will depend on the variety as some naturally grow earlier than others. The sticks should be pulled, not cut, and you simply hold the stalk near the base and pull it away from the crown. Never pull all the sticks from the clump in one go as it weakens the plant. Continue to pull little and often through the summer, as needed. Traditionally, the rhubarb season finishes at the end of July, but some of the late varieties can be pulled through August. After this time, allow the stalks and foliage to carry on growing to build up the crown for next year.

Above: Cutting off the rhubarb flower stem.
Right: Clearing away dead foliage in autumn.

Pest and diseases

When grown in good conditions, rhubarb doesn't suffer from too many problems but there are a couple to look out for.

Slugs and snails – These can be a problem in early spring and they will nibble at the new growth as it emerges. They can also be a problem under forcing pots where it is dark and moist.

Crown rot – This can be a problem especially in very wet soil conditions. The crown buds and root tissue rot. Growth is weak and stalks die back to the crown. There are no treatments available, so avoid growing in wet conditions and keep the plants strong by feeding in the growing season.

Honey fungus – Rhubarb roots can be attacked by this fungus which is a soil-borne fungus. Tell-tale signs are wilting stalks and white mycelium (fungal growth) in the dead tissue on the crown. Honey-coloured toadstools may also appear in autumn. There is no treatment and affected plants should be dug out.

Rhubarb in the kitchen

I love the first, rosy-pink stems of forced rhubarb - it's always a sign to me that the new season is on its way. As much as I love the hearty veg that we eat over the winter, the first rhubarb sticks are like a breath of fresh air. So tender, delicate and tasty. Of course, it has a slight sourness but I always think that can help wake the taste buds up in time for all the new flavours about to burst into the kitchen.

Martin used to get a bowl of sugar for his rhubarb dunking but my Mum got us to make a greaseproof paper cone which we'd put sugar in and then happily wander around nibbling and dunking some forced rhubarb for ages! Not good for the teeth, of course, but very tasty.

Rhubarb heaven

Rhubarb is, though, really good for bone protection as it's high in calcium, so when added to dairy products, rhubarb is positively a superfood! That's my excuse for indulging in this quick cook pud - plus it tastes good too!

Serves 4

Only takes about 10 minutes, but best made ahead to give the flavours time to blend together

Ingredients

- 3-4 sticks early rhubarb
- 50g caster sugar
- 1 dessertspoon water
- 2 small cartons plain yoghurt
- 200ml carton crème fraiche
- 2 bulbs stem ginger, diced
- 2 tblsps light muscovado sugar

Method

- Cut the rhubarb into 2cm slices. Pop in a pan with the water and sugar and simmer over a low heat until the sugar has dissolved.
- Cover and simmer for about 7 minutes until the rhubarb is just tender. Leave to one side to cool.
- Mix the crème fraiche and yoghurt together in a bowl and stir in the chopped ginger.
- Layer the rhubarb and yoghurt mixture in your serving dishes, leveling the top of the final creamy layer.
- Sprinkle with the muscovado sugar and pop in the fridge for at least an hour. The sugar will dissolve and leave a lovely, sweet topping.

Rhubarb and ginger turnovers

This is a bit more of an indulgent sweet treat but great served hot with custard on a crisp spring day.

Makes 4

Takes about 45 minutes plus chilling time

Ingredients

1 large Bramley apple, peeled, cored and diced
Knob of butter
2 tblsps caster sugar
3 or 4 sticks pink forced rhubarb, cut into 1cm pieces
2 tblsps water
Pinch of powdered ginger
2 small balls stem ginger from a jar, chopped finely
1 x 375g pack puff pastry, ready rolled sheets
1 small egg, beaten
Extra caster sugar for sprinkling
A little butter for greasing

Method

- Put the apple into a pan along with the butter and cook over a gentle heat for 3 or 4 minutes until just softening. Add the water and the rhubarb then sprinkle in the ginger powder and continue to cook gently for about 4 minutes, but don't let the rhubarb lose its bite or shape.
- Strain in a sieve over a bowl, reserving the juices.
- Remove the pastry from the fridge, (usually 20 minutes before using but follow

the packet instructions) and unroll. Cut the pastry into 4 equal rectangles and place on a baking sheet.

- Put a large spoonful of the rhubarb and apple on each rectangle. Place it on one half, keeping it away from the edges. There will be some fruit left over so keep to one side.
- Scatter the chopped stem ginger over the top of the fruit.
- Brush around the sides of the pastry with some of the beaten egg and fold the pastry over. Firm down lightly to get rid of any large air pockets and press the edges together. Use the end of a teaspoon or a fork to seal the edges really well and trim with a sharp knife to neaten, then pop them in the fridge for 30 minutes or so to firm the pastry up.
- Brush all over with some of the remaining beaten egg and put in the oven, 200°C (fan 180°C), gas 6, for 15 minutes until just starting to rise and turning golden brown. Working very quickly, remove from the oven, brush with a little more egg and sprinkle with the extra sugar. Return to the oven for another 10–15 minutes until golden brown and well risen. Don't worry too much if some of the juices have leaked out as it makes a crispy finish to the edges of the pastry.
- Whilst they're cooking, pour the juices from the apple and rhubarb into a small saucepan and bring to a rapid boil. Reduce down to thick syrup then pour onto any leftover fruit and keep warm to serve with the turnovers.
- Serve the turnovers whilst they're still warm. Put on the plate with the spare fruit and serve with some sweetened crème fraiche or pour over some hot custard.

Quick cook – Rhubarb and apple sauce to serve with pork

Serves 2–3

Only takes 15 minutes

Ingredients

3 medium stalks of rhubarb, cut into bite-sized pieces
1 Bramley apple, peeled, cored and diced
3 tsps brown sugar
3 tblsps runny honey
2 tblsps cider vinegar
1 tsp cinnamon

Method

- Cook the rhubarb and cooking apple together in a saucepan with the other ingredients until tender then lightly blend together.
- Use to serve alongside roast pork or pork chops.

Easy no cook – Rhubarb salsa

Try making a punchy salsa to serve with cold meats by dicing some just-cooked rhubarb, peppers and spring onions then mixing with some chilli, chopped coriander, brown sugar to taste and a good squeeze of lime juice.

Quick no cook - Ginger spiced rhubarb

Break up a ginger biscuit and put in the bottom of a ramekin. Splash over a dash of either fresh orange juice or Cointreau and leave to soak in for a few minutes. Mix together a good tablespoon of whipped double cream (or low-fat yoghurt) and the same of rhubarb purée, then spoon over the top of the biscuit. Leave in the fridge for about an hour to blend the flavours.

Quick cook - Rhubarb mess

Use some cooled, roasted pink rhubarb instead of strawberries in this classic meringue and cream dish.

Jill's tips

- Rhubarb freezes really well so I try to keep picking in big batches. I usually cook mine first and then freeze it in small, ready-to-use portions.
- Roasting brings out the flavours of both types of rhubarb and cooking couldn't be easier – trim the stalks into 2.5cm pieces and pack them into an ovenproof dish. Scatter over the zest of an orange and a bit of diced root ginger. Then sprinkle with some sugar, either caster or soft brown, and add about a tablespoon of water and some orange juice. Roast in a moderate oven, 170°C (fan 150°C), gas 3, for about 10 minutes for forced rhubarb and a bit longer for main crop until just tender but not mushy.
- Then you have the basis for loads of puddings! We often just pile the cooled rhubarb onto some vanilla ice cream or swirl it into some plain yoghurt.
- For a smoother texture, I pop the forced rhubarb into the blender and get a lovely, smooth, rosy-pink purée which I can freeze or use straight away.

Rhubarb gingerbread

I really should include some ideas for main-crop rhubarb although you can probably guess that I prefer the forced variety!

This is a fantastic ginger cake using main-crop rhubarb that keeps really well - in fact, it gets better with age.

Cuts into 12 pieces

Takes about an hour plus cooling time

Ingredients

50g butter
50g caster sugar
1½ tblsps black treacle
100g plain flour
½ tsp bicarbonate of soda
1 good tsp ground ginger
1 egg, beaten
Milk to add
125g (about 2 small sticks) rhubarb, diced into small pieces
75g crystallised ginger, chopped

Greased and fully lined 19cm shallow, square sponge tin

Method

- Preheat your oven to 180°C (fan 160°C), gas 4.
- Put the butter, sugar and treacle into a medium-sized pan and heat gently, stirring until the butter has melted and everything is combined. Leave to cool for a few minutes.
- Sift together the flour, bicarbonate of soda and ginger powder. Add to the mixture in the pan, stirring well.
- Add the beaten egg and begin to mix together. Add about a tablespoon of milk and continue to mix until everything is incorporated. Add a little more milk until it reaches a soft, dropping consistency.
- Spoon 2 good tablespoons into the tin and spread out with the back of the spoon to cover the base.
- Scatter the rhubarb evenly over the mix then top with the crystallised ginger.
- Spoon over the remaining gingerbread mixture, trying to coat as much of the rhubarb as possible. Don't worry if it doesn't cover it all - the mix will rise during baking and cover the filling.

- Pop in the oven and bake for 45–50 minutes. The cake will be dark brown, firm to the touch and a skewer will come out clean after inserting. Leave to cool in the tin for 10 minutes then put onto a wire rack.
- Peel off the paper when cool and cut into squares to serve.

Strawberries in the garden

Strawberries are probably one of the easiest fruits to grow, with the promise of red, juicy fruits just a few months after planting. Traditionally, strawberries are grown in the ground, but they are also ideal for growing in a wide range of containers – in fact, I now grow all our strawberries in hanging baskets or pots and troughs. This allows me to bring them into the greenhouse or polytunnel for an early crop. Even without any heat in the polytunnel, the fruits ripen a couple of weeks earlier than outside.

Young strawberry plants (runners) are readily available from mail-order companies and are usually sold as bare-root plants ready for autumn or spring planting. Garden centres and nurseries also sell strawberry plants from spring onwards and these are usually small potted plants. Both types should be disease and virus free to ensure the plants grow away without any problems. If you are starting from scratch, it is always advisable to start with clean stock as old and virus-infected plants produce a poor crop. Strawberry plants are not expensive to buy and the crop that you will harvest over the next two or three years will more than pay for the plants.

Soil conditions

A strawberry bed will be productive for three or four years, so make sure the soil is prepared by removing all perennial weeds and work in plenty of well-rotted organic matter. Ideally, the soil should drain freely to encourage good root growth and to help prevent soil-borne diseases, which are often a problem in waterlogged soils.

If you have a wet, heavy clay soil, it is worth creating a raised bed to grow the strawberries in. Filled with a mix of good topsoil and compost, you will get plenty of healthy growth and fruit.

When growing in containers as I do now, mix up a compost of two thirds multipurpose and one

Varieties

There are many varieties of strawberries to choose from and by planting several types, you can increase the length of the picking season. Some also have attractive foliage or different coloured flowers and can be used as part of an ornamental display.

'Florence' – A late-summer variety that has good disease resistance and a heavy crop of dark-red berries well into July.

Top, left: Potting rooted strawberry runners into a hanging pot
Right: Peg down healthy runners into pots of compost to root.
Bottom left: Planting strawberries into troughs.
Right: Liquid feed as the fruits start to develop.

third loam-based compost which will keep the plants growing for two or three years.

Planting

Planting can be done in early autumn using new runners or new plants propagated from existing plants. If you plant in early September, the plants will have time to settle in and establish over the winter and come spring, they will grow away, flower and fruit.

You can also now buy cold-stored runners for planting from spring through until mid-summer. These are bare-root runners lifted in autumn and then stored in a chiller at -2°C. Cold-stored runners planted in spring will produce a crop around sixty days after planting as long as they are watered to help them establish. Many young potted strawberry plants sold in garden centres in spring are cold-stored runners so will also establish very quickly after planting.

For the garden, plant approximately 30cm-35cm (12in-14in) apart in all directions in holes deep enough to accommodate the root system, but do not bury the top growth bud (crown) below the soil level. Make sure the plants are firmed in and watered to settle the soil around the roots.

Planting in containers

Planting times for containers are the same as for planting outside and it is important to make sure autumn runners establish before winter. Generally speaking, you space the plants closer in troughs or large pots. I plant approximately

'Elvira' – An early summer variety that produces a heavy yield of large, firm fruits and shows some resistance to powdery mildew. It also has a very good flavour.

'Elsanta' – A popular variety with commercial growers and the home gardener. A reliable cropper with good flavour.

'Alice' – Flowers over a longer period and produces fruits throughout June and into July. Has very sweet fruits and good disease resistance.

'Cambridge Favourite' – An old variety that is still popular with many gardeners. It produces medium-sized berries with a good flavour and is resistant to powdery mildew.

'Vivarosa' – A pink-flowering strawberry that is ideal for containers and hanging baskets. The red fruits are medium size and have a good flavour.

15cm (6in) apart.

A very simple method of growing just a few strawberry plants is to use a hanging basket. In a 30cm–35cm (12in–14in) basket, you only need three plants that are evenly spaced around the top of the basket. From just three plants in a basket, you should get a few bowls of strawberries in early summer.

Aftercare

After planting in a container or basket, keep the compost just moist and only water when the compost starts to dry out and gradually increase as new growth is made.

If you want early fruits, bring the containers of strawberries under cover around February. As soon as fruits start to develop, feed weekly with a high-potash fertiliser liquid feed. This will help the fruits to swell and ripen.

Plants in the garden should be kept weed free and watered in dry weather. When the flowers start to open in mid to late spring, protect the blossoms from frost by draping fleece over the plants. Flowers that have been frosted will have a black centre and will not develop into fruits. At this point, outside plants can be fed with a general fertiliser to encourage the fruits to develop. To protect fruits from soil splash, you can spread straw between the plants.

From June onwards, the plants will start to develop runners and ideally these should be removed on a regular basis unless you want to save a few to produce new plants.

Once the fruits have been picked, trim back the old foliage to soil level and continue to feed and water the plants. A new set of leaves will quickly develop to form bushy plants.

In autumn, stop watering plants in containers as there is usually enough rain to keep the plants ticking over. Although strawberry plants are hardy, it is a good idea to stand the containers against a south-facing wall or place them in a cold greenhouse to prevent the roots from freezing during winter.

In early spring as new growth starts to emerge, tidy up the plants by removing any dead or yellow leaves and apply a general fertiliser to the compost to replace lost nutrients.

'Golden Alexandria' – An attractive alpine strawberry that is very easy to grow from seed. The foliage is yellow and produces neat clump-forming plants. Small, sweet fruits are produced all summer long and well into the autumn.

Top: Planting young strawberry plants.
Centre: Hoeing between plants to chop off weeds.
Bottom: Trimming back old leaves after the plants have fruited.

Harvesting

This is the best part and picking strawberries is always a pleasant job. The main advantage of growing your own is that you can allow the fruits to fully ripen to a deep-red colour. When ripe, they have so much more flavour and sweetness, unlike some supermarket strawberries that are like bullets with no taste! Once the fruits start to ripen, check the plants every few days and pick when they are at their best.

Pest and diseases

Vine weevils – These can sometimes be a problem and during the winter months it is well worth checking the pots for small, cream-coloured grubs that eat the roots. If found, control with nematodes from spring onwards when the conditions are warmer.

Powdery mildew – This is a fungal disease that causes a white powdery coating on the leaves. It tends to attack plants that are short of water as a result of dry weather, so regular watering and feeding will help.

Aphids – Can also be a problem in late spring and they feed by sucking the sap from the new leaves, which can cause distortion and spread viruses. Where you only have a few plants, the aphids can be rubbed off by hand or controlled with a suitable insecticide.

Slugs – These love ripening strawberries and even if the plants are being grown in containers, they are still prone to attack. If slugs are a problem in your garden, you need to take precautions as soon as the berries are fully formed.

Birds – Can also be a problem as they peck at ripening fruits. A piece of netting draped over the fruits whilst they are ripening will protect them.

Grey mould (Botrytis) – Another fungal disease that is easily recognised as the fruits develop a mould on them. It often starts as a result of slug or bird damage or if the weather conditions are wet and warm. Avoid overcrowding the plants to allow better air circulation.

Martin's tip

Although it's advisable to start with new, virus free plants, you can produce more plants from your existing strawberries as long as they are growing healthily. Leaving the runners attached to the parent plant simply peg a few down into trays or pots of potting compost. In a very short time, roots will develop and the new plants can then be severed from the parent plant. However, if the original strawberry plants have mottled or distorted leaves, do not propagate from them as they may have a virus.

Below: Grey mould developing on the fruits.

Strawberries in the kitchen

I'm forever grateful that Martin's not into sport! The World Cup passes us by and we only watch cricket when the local team reaches the final! However, I have always had a soft spot for Wimbledon and try to watch bits when I can – the highlights in the evening, of course, as any spare daytime in June is spent in the garden! And, of course, its association with strawberries is well known so any excuse to eat more of the fruits is fine with me!

We always grow some strawberries under cover for an early crop and it's a real treat to go into the greenhouse and help myself to a handful of strawberries before anything else is really ready in the garden. The children used to love them too – in fact, Aimee, our eldest, has always tried to grow strawberries wherever she's lived, from being a student until now, living in New Zealand.

Strawberry and chocolate muffins with strawberry cheesecake topping and chocolate-dipped strawberries

This is a perfect treat to serve up while you're watching the Wimbledon finals. These buns are most delicious eaten fresh but will keep in the fridge for eating the next day.

Makes 12 muffins

Takes about 35 minutes

Ingredients

For the muffins:

- 125g butter (room temperature)
- 125g caster sugar
- 2 eggs
- 85g self raising flour
- ¼ tsp baking powder
- 40g cocoa powder
- 1-2 tblsps milk

For the topping:

200g full-fat Philadelphia cheese
200g icing sugar, sifted
150g strawberries

For decoration:

About 100g dark or milk chocolate
3 strawberries, cut into quarters
12 strawberries for dipping

Method

For the dipped strawberries:

› Try to use strawberries with the stalks left on for dipping. Lay a piece of greaseproof paper on a flat tray.
› Break about three quarters of the chocolate up and melt in a bowl over a pan of gently simmering water. Carefully dip the strawberries into the chocolate, rolling them around until covered to halfway up the fruit.
› Leave to set on the greaseproof paper then remove and keep in a cool place.

For the muffins:

› Line a muffin tin with paper cases.
› Put the butter and sugar into a large bowl and cream together with an electric mixer until light and fluffy. Gradually add the eggs, one at a time, and beat in well. Add a little of the flour if the mixture looks as if it's about to split.
› Sift together the flour, baking powder and cocoa then fold gently into the mixture. Add a little of the milk to make a soft, dropping consistency.
› Pile the mixture into the muffin cases and pop into the oven, 190°C (fan 170°C) gas 5, for about 15 minutes until risen and just firm to the touch.
› Leave to cool.

For the topping:

› Hull the strawberries and cut in half. Pop in a liquidiser and blitz until puréed. Pass through a sieve to remove the seeds if they bother you.
› Beat the cream cheese and icing sugar together until smooth and creamy then gradually fold in the strawberry purée. The mixture needs to be thick enough to spread so only add enough to give a good colour, taste and thickness.
› Keep in the fridge until ready to use.
› When the muffins are cool, I like to peel off the paper cases but you could leave them on. Spread the topping over the top of each muffin then top with a quarter of a strawberry. Grate some of the leftover chocolate over the top to finish off.

Serve with the chocolate-dipped strawberries and any leftover purée.

Quick no cook - Strawberry dressing

Make a strawberry salad dressing to add to a chicken salad - in a blender, mix 2 parts oil and 1 part vinegar with 2 good handfuls of strawberries, some chopped red onion and a dash of Dijon mustard. Blitz until smooth.

Quick cook - Strawberry cream

Make a strawberry vanilla cream - whip some double cream along with the seeds from a vanilla pod then add some diced strawberries and stir through. Perfect on top of a pavlova or with scones.

Jill's tips

- Always eat strawberries at room temperature, preferably chopped, scattered with a little caster sugar after being left to stand for half an hour. The juices will be starting to appear and the fruits will be perfect to enjoy.
- Make a quick and easy purée by chopping up some strawberries and stirring in some caster sugar. Leave for half an hour to let the fruits soften a little then push through a sieve. Use to top ice cream or to pour as a dressing.

Easy no cook - Strawberry salsa

Now this recipe isn't strictly from the garden but it's one of our favourites on a warm summer's evening if we're having some spicy Mexican food.

For a really delicious salsa to serve with some tortilla chips, try dicing and mixing a small bowl of strawberries, half a mango, half a red onion, 1 avocado, some chilli and chopped fresh parsley in a large bowl. Add some runny honey and a good squeeze of lime juice to taste.

Index

C

R

S

T